Consumers Digest®
AUTOMOTIVE ADVISOR

D1089103

Consumers Digest® AUTOMOTIVE ADVISOR

The Car Owner's A-to-Z Reference to
Maintenance and Repair

THOMAS J. BEAM

illustrated by
Edward R. Lipinski

foreword by
Brian Buckta,
BRAUN'S R&D SERVICES

Lebhar-Friedman Books

NEW YORK CHICAGO LOS ANGELES LONDON PARIS TOKYO

©2000 Lebhar-Friedman Books

Published by Lebhar-Friedman Books
Lebhar-Friedman Books is a company of Lebhar-Friedman Inc.
Visit our Internet site at www.lf.books.com

Printed in the United States of America

Consumers Digest is a registered trademark of Consumers Digest, Inc.

Beam, Thomas J.,
    Consumers digest automotive advisor / Thomas J. Beam.
        p.   cm.
    Includes index.
    ISBN 0-86730-807-9 (alk. paper.)
    1. Automobiles—Dictionaries. I. Title.

TL9 .B36 2000
629.2'03—dc21

00-0282378

All automotive repair and maintenance tasks should be performed with
safety precautions. Lebhar-Friedman Books are not liable for any legal
action arising from readers suffering injury when following the directions
in this book.

Consumers Digest
AUTOMOTIVE ADVISOR

CONTENTS

A

B

Within the main entries, a subitem may be printed
in SMALL CAPITAL LETTERS, indicating that there is
further information on that subject as a main entry.

The Automobile–An American Institution

From the original "horse-less carriage" to the high-tech machines of today, nothing has influenced the American way of life quite like the automobile. We live in an incredibly mobile society, driving our cars virtually everywhere we go. From an airplane it's easy to see how our landscape is divided and outlined with seemingly endless strips of neatly arranged cement and asphalt, all providing an automotive link to anywhere we want to travel. In an average urban area, the daily accumulative amount of miles driven easily reaches into the millions. Cars have become so much a part of our culture that they have even become a reference point for our identity. It would be highly unlikely, for example, to see a senior citizen in a high-performance two-seater sports car. It would be just as unlikely to see a wealthy man driving an early model used car that is showing signs of its age. An individual with a family is more likely to be seen driving a station wagon, mini-van, or S.U.V.

The average person will invest a large portion of their annual income in car-related expenses. This includes everything from gasoline and oil to insurance, service, and accessories. The jobs provided by automobile manufacturing, service, and support infrastructures has provided our economy with a major portion of the revenue that we, in turn, re-invest in our automobiles. Cars provide us with a sense of safety, security, and freedom. We insure our cars, we wash our cars, we wax and polish our cars. We even sing songs about our cars. We could go on and on with endless examples of how the automobile has influenced our society, and the honeymoon is far from over.

Consumers Digest Automotive Advisor is an indispensable A-to-Z overview of what makes up a car. It provides, in an encyclopedic format, descriptions and explanations of every car component and at the same time, shares expert tips and maintenance advice on how to keep those parts—and your entire car—running to the best of their ability. Using this book as an invaluable reference tool will empower you with the knowledge and wherewithal to understand what your automotive technician is telling you. If you have a problem with your alternator, just look up under "A" and read all about what an alternator does and how it fits into the general framework of a car. It's that easy. But before you delve into the nuts and bolts of the book, let's take a short drive down memory lane and see how the automobile has taken us through the twentieth century and into the new millennium.

A Brief Automotive Timeline

1885 ◾ Karl Benz produced the first production car.

1893 ◾ The Office of Road Inquiry opened. This agency became the Federal Highway Administration in 1967.

1908 ◾ Ford introduced the Model "T." Prior to this time, car ownership was reserved for the wealthy elite. The model "T" made the automobile affordable and available to the general public. Fifteen million were produced over the next nineteen years.

MODEL "T" FORD 1909

1912 ■ The electric starter was introduced. Prior to this time, driving was a man's job. It took a man's strength to turn the crank to start the car engine. The electric starter opened the world of driving to women.

1927 ■ Ford introduced the Model "A." Prior to the Model "A," cars with creature comforts and aesthetics were mainly reserved for the wealthy elite. The Model "A" was a step up from the basic transportation that the Model "T" provided. Although several auto makers made similar "affordable" cars, the Model "A" was the most popular car in its class.

1939 ■ Four-wheel drive was developed—introduced in 1940. This was the predecessor of today's four-wheel drive sport utility vehicles.

1948 ■ The first fully automatic transmission was offered. Prior to this, driving with a manual transmission required an increased level of skill and ability. The automatic transmission is one of many convenient features that make driving easier for us today.

1952 ■ Power brakes were introduced.

1953 ■ Power steering was introduced. Prior to the introduction of power steering, driving required a certain level of physical strength. Power steering eliminated that requirement.

1956 ■ Construction of the Eisenhower Interstate system begins. This was the advent of the mobile society we have today. Prior to this time, auto travel was done on two-lane highways with lots of "stop-and-go" interruptions. The Interstate highway system changed our cultural view of travel, as these new roads made it possible to travel long distances with ease. Subsequently, auto sales soared to new records in the late 1950s and early 1960s.

1965 ■ The transistor ignition system was introduced. This was just the first in a long series of advances in automotive ignition system technology.

1965 ■ Pollution controls were introduced on cars in California. This was another first in a long series of advances in automotive pollution (emission) controls technology.

1975 ■ Electronic ignition systems became standard equipment. Prior to electronic ignition, frequent replacement of ignition components was necessary. Solid-state electronic ignition eliminated the need for frequent ignition replacement service.

1980 ■ On-board computers with limited diagnostic capabilities appeared. These were the predecessors to the high-tech on-board computers of today.

1985 ■ Cars sold in California were required to have OBD-I (On-board Diagnostics–First Generation) computers. The rest of the nation was soon to follow.

1996 ■ All cars were required to have OBD-II computers programmed to meet United States Environmental Protection Agency (EPA) specifications. There is more computer intelligence on-board these cars than there was on-board the NASA moon missions.

1997 ■ Alternative fuel technology hybrid vehicles were scheduled for production. These vehicles are designed to run on a variable combination of gasoline and ethanol. As our petroleum supply decreases, we will depend more upon alternative fuel technology for affordable transportation.

Remember your first car?... Safety First

It may have been a hand-me-down from a relative, a fixer-upper, or maybe it was even a sports car or brand-new model. It doesn't really matter what it was. What was important was that it was yours. Your first car meant freedom. It was a certain sign of maturity and "coming of age." Remember the magical feeling of driving down the road alone in your car for the first time? It was like having your own personal key that would open the door to new and exciting places you had never been before.

Your first car also brought on a whole new set of responsibilities as a car owner. The first and most important responsibility we have as car owners is safety. Although auto manufacturers have taken a great deal

SAFETY RESPONSIBILITY

- Safely operational engine and transmission
- Safely operational brakes
- Safely operational steering
- Safe tires with adequate tread
- Safely operational exhaust system
- Adequate rear-view mirrors
- Functional headlights, tail-lights, and warning lights
- Functional audible warning device (car horn)
- Clear visibility through clean windows
- Adequate passenger safety (seat belts are mandated by law in several states)
- On-board emergency equipment

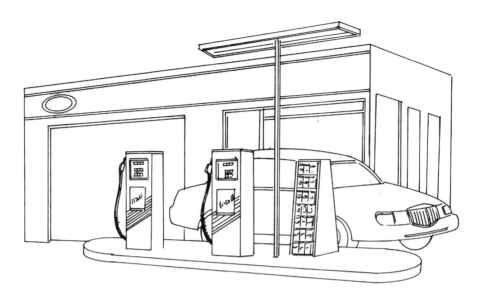

of initiative in designing and building cars to meet stringent safety standards, increasing levels of traffic increase the need for additional safety measures. As more and more cars continue to enter our roadways, our government is heavily addressing key automotive safety issues. Much of this legislation is focused on insurance-related issues to safeguard responsible drivers.

With all of the progress that has been made toward auto safety, car owners still have the ultimate social responsibility to keep their car safe and roadworthy for themselves and their community.

To accommodate safety responsibilities, car owners have a social responsibility to maintain their cars, and to quickly repair any safety-related problems. As a car ages it may still start well, run well, and serve its general purpose. But without vigilant maintenance it is only a matter of time before it will require major repair. It is much easier and less expensive to avoid a major repair if possible. This can be facilitated with frequent visual inspections and a regular maintenance schedule according to your manufacturer's recommendations. Preventative maintenance will also extend the life of your car and increase its resale value.

Car owners also have a social responsibility to our environment. When a car is brand new, it runs cleanly and pollutes very little. Again, as a car ages it may still start well, run well, and serve its general purpose. But without vigilant maintenance it will become less and less environmentally friendly. Two key areas of automotive environmental impact include:

Leaks

A car uses a variety of fluids. When these fluids leak from our cars, they end up in our water. They will show up first as annoying spots on the driveway. When it rains, automotive fluids are washed off the pavement and into storm sewers, lakes, and rivers. One gallon of leaking automotive fluid has the potential to contaminate up to one million gallons of drinking water. When we add more fluid to replenish what was lost, we only repeat the cycle—until we fix the leak. When we fix automotive leaks, it's a win/win for the environment and for our wallet—automotive fluids aren't cheap.

Emissions

Automotive emissions are responsible for an estimated 50 percent of ground-level ozone pollution in urban areas. Federal environmental test procedures assure that a car's emissions are at an acceptable level when it leaves the showroom floor. After that, it is up to the car owner to maintain the emission control equipment that makes this possible. Many urban areas across the nation are mandated by U.S. EPA regulations to test cars on a regular basis to validate the operation of emission control equipment. A clean running car is another win/win for the environment and for the car owner who is reaping the benefits of maximum fuel economy and lowered operating costs.

The Auto Repair Technician of the New Millennium

The era of the "shade-tree mechanic" has long passed as the automotive industry has moved rapidly into the technological age. To be competitive in today's high-tech auto repair community, today's automotive technician must have a broad base of knowledge in a variety of areas.

Today's automotive technician is more like an automotive "physician," with a functional level of training and experience to fulfill the roles of:

- Mechanical Engineer
- Safety Engineer
- Electrician
- Plumber
- Welder and Metal Fabricator
- Metallurgist
- Lubrication Engineer
- Chemist

- Physicist
- Painter
- Hazardous Waste Handler
- Computer Analyst
- Electronics Engineer
- Psychologist
- Business Manager

Like today's physicians, today's auto technicians have general training and knowledge in many areas, but are likely to specialize in a particular area. Some possible specialty areas include:

- Wheel Alignment/Tires
- Brakes/Exhaust
- Electrical Repair
- Interior Repairs
- Electronic (Computer-related) Repairs

- Heavy Engine Repair and Replacement
- Transmission Repair and Replacement
- Cosmetics/Body Repairs

Prior to specializing, a fully trained technician has invested in an average of four years of formal education coupled with hands-on experience. And a technician's education never ends. Today's new and rapidly changing automotive technology presents additional ongoing training needs. To stay current with changing technology, a professional automotive technician will also invest more than two full weeks each year learning about new automotive technology service and repair procedures.

In addition to the time and effort your technician invests in their trade, an average technician also has several thousand dollars invested in basic tools and equipment. It is not uncommon for a specialized technician to have tens of thousands of dollars invested in specialty equipment. Not including building and property costs, an average independent repair shop will have well over $100,000 invested in tools and equipment to service and repair today's high-tech autos.

The Doctor is IN

When we are sick, we visit the doctor, but the doctor doesn't treat us before he investigates our illness. A thorough diagnosis is needed before treatment can begin. The same thing is true in today's automotive repair industry. When our car is "sick," a technician must first make an accurate diagnosis before they begin repairs.

When we first see the doctor, the doctor begins by asking a lot of questions to get an idea of what might be wrong. The more complete information the doctor receives, the easier it is for the doctor to make an accurate diagnosis. Again, the same is true in today's auto repair industry—the better the information your technician receives, the easier and more cost-effective it will be to diagnose and repair the problem.

Once the initial information is gathered, the doctor will usually do an examination. At this point the doctor may even order some specialized tests that will target a specific area to gather the information necessary to complete a full diagnosis of the illness. And once again, the same theory is true with today's auto repair industry. A properly trained and equipped auto technician will always use some form of diagnostic testing to confirm a suspected diagnosis.

Once an accurate diagnosis is made, the problem still needs to be treated. This often requires additional skills, knowledge, and specialized tools and equipment. If so equipped, your technician may proceed

INFORMATION GATHERING

In addition to keeping a written service and repair record, some of the information that is particularly helpful for your technician includes:

- What is the car doing specifically?
- Does it happen when the temperature is hot or cold?
- Does it happen on the first start of the day, or does it happen all day long?
- Does it happen at idle, at cruise, or at specific speeds?
- Is the "check engine" light on?
- When was the last time it was emission tested, and did it pass?
- When was the last time the car was worked on, and what was done to it?
- Does the car have any leaks, and what colors are they?
- Does the car overheat easily?
- Are there any problems with exterior lights (headlights, tail-lights, warning lights)?
- Are there any problems with interior lights (dash panel, courtesy lights)?
- Was an aftermarket (not original equipment) accessory recently installed?
- Are there any problems with electric windows or door locks?
- Do you hear noise when you brake or coast?
- Do you hear noise when you are in park, in gear, or in neutral?
- Do you hear noise at idle speeds, or at higher speeds?
- Do you hear noise when you turn a corner, or when you are going straight?
- As a courtesy to your technician, are there any special instructions they should have before they take your car for a test-drive?

with the repair, or your technician may refer you to a specialist. A quality cost-effective automotive repair has four main ingredients:

Quality Technician

Once again, the era of the shade-tree mechanic is long gone. Choose your auto technician as wisely as you would choose a health specialist. If you have a problem with your heart, you will want to visit a heart specialist. If you have a problem with your car's transmission, you will want to visit an automotive transmission specialist. The National Institution for Automotive Service Excellence (ASE) is an organization that certifies today's automotive technicians in a wide variety of professional automotive applications. To become ASE certified in a particular area, an auto technician must demonstrate proficiency in that area by preparing for and passing long, intense, thorough written examinations.

Although auto technicians are not required to have ASE certification, the effort required to take this step speaks volumes about the professional dedication of the technician. An ASE Master Technician is certified in all of the general automotive repair categories, much like the general practitioner physician. An ASE Master Technician will often have additional ASE certifications pertaining to their specialty area.

Quality Information

Once again, the better and more complete the information your technician receives, the easier and more cost-effective it will be to diagnose and repair the problem. Quality information provides a higher degree of efficiency in accurate diagnosis, creating a win/win for the technician and for the car owner who is paying for the service.

Quality Parts

A properly trained technician knows that the repair will always only be as good as the parts. Although there is an initial savings with a less expensive part, it will probably end up costing more in the long run if the part needs to be replaced again later. It pays to follow the advice of a trained technician. The parts supplied by your technician were chosen for reliability, and will usually carry an outstanding warranty. A specialized technician will also have specialized parts knowledge in their particular specialty area.

Quality Tools and Equipment

A properly trained and equipped technician has made a significant investment in tools and equipment. They know that there is always the "right" tool for the "right" job. In trained hands, quality, reliable, professional-grade tooling makes it quicker, easier, and safer for the technician to diagnose and properly repair your car. This is a win/win for the technician and for the car owner who is paying for efficient, safe auto repair.

The Anatomy of the Automobile

Much like the human body, today's automobile consists of a myriad of complex systems that are finely tuned to work together toward a common goal. Everything in today's high-tech automobile has a specific purpose. Your car may be able to run adequately without certain components in place, but it will only be a matter of time before a failure occurs. To assure that everything is working properly, it is important that we take our car for regular "check-ups." There is no technical correlation between the car starting and running, and how well and safe it is. As a car ages it may still look well, start well, run well, and serve its general purpose. But it may have a hidden illness that is lurking beneath the surface, much like the way "the silent killer," high blood pressure, can attack our physical health. Basically, there are five major anatomical systems of the automobile, and they all interact and work together to provide us with safe, reliable transportation.

Underhood

This is the "thorax" of the automobile. The auto underhood contains the vehicle engine and all of the supporting components that provide the horsepower to propel the car. Most of this horsepower is used to move the car from a stationary "stopped" position to cruising speed. Once a car is up to speed it requires relatively little horsepower to maintain the speed, with the exceptions of steep uphill grades and heavy wind resistance. Your car's underhood was designed to supply power for specific loads and specific operating conditions. To extend the service life of your car, it is important to adhere to your auto manufacturer's instructions regarding these issues.

Your car's underhood section includes such major components as:

- Engine
- Alternator
- Starter
- Battery
- Ignition System
- Cooling System
- Air-conditioning Compressor
- Some Pollution (Emission) Controls
- Power Steering and Power Brake Components

Undercar

This section represents the "skeleton" and the "legs" of the automobile. Automotive undercar components work in conjunction with the underhood to safely and efficiently propel and steer your car. The "skeleton" holds the car together and provides safe handling and comfortable travel.

The "skeleton" portion of the undercar includes such major components as:

- Frame
- Springs
- Shock Absorbers/Struts
- Steering Mechanisms
- Exhaust
- Gas Tank
- Heat Shields and Air Dams

The "legs" provide the safe transmission of power from the underhood to the drive wheels. The major components included in the "legs" section of the automotive undercar include:

- Transmission
- Drive Gears and Axles
- Brakes
- Tires and Wheels

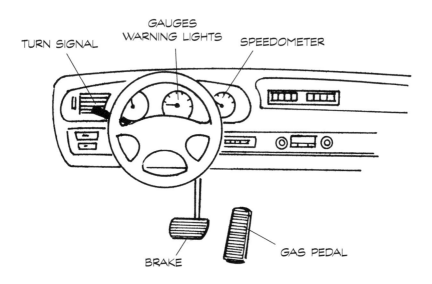

Interior

The interior is where we find the "brains" of today's automobile. Although today's cars are highly computerized, they still won't drive themselves. The interior contains all of the equipment we need to drive safely. This includes such major components as:

- Steering Wheel
- Seats
- Safety Belts
- Airbag
- Ignition/Starter Switch
- Transmission Gear-shift
- Speedometer
- Gauges or Engine Warning Lights
- Gas pedal
- Brake pedal
- Turn Signal Lever
- Horn Switch
- On-Board Computer Control

The interior section also includes some components that provide us with comfort and entertainment. This includes such components as:

- Radio
- Heater Core and Air Conditioning Evaporator Coil (behind the dashboard)

INTERIOR SEATS
STEERING WHEEL
AIR BAGS

Exterior

This is the "skin" of the automobile. The exterior protects the vehicle and its occupants from the elements while it provides safety, aerodynamic efficiency, and aesthetics.

The major components in the automotive exterior include:

- Windows
- Hood and Trunk
- Fenders
- Headlights
- Tail-lights and Warning Lights

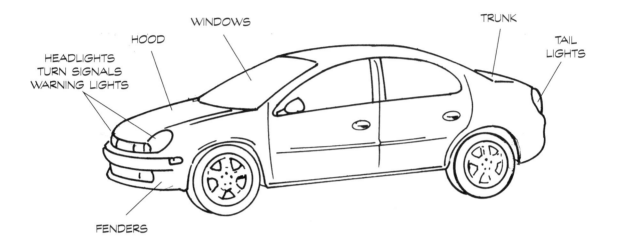

HEADLIGHTS
TURN SIGNALS
WARNING LIGHTS

HOOD

WINDOWS

TRUNK

TAIL
LIGHTS

FENDERS

Wiring

This is the "nervous system" of the automobile. The wiring system is intricately laced throughout the car to provide power and to transmit signals. There are two sections within the wiring system. The first section is electrical. The electrical section provides the power necessary to run various components and accessories, from the headlights to the tail-lights and everything in-between. This section includes a wide array of specialized switches, fuses, and transformers to accomplish its tasks.

The second section of the wiring system is the electronic system. This system is often referred to as the On-board Diagnostic (OBD) system. This system consists of a centralized computer that is programmed with specific information regarding your car's specifically designed operation and performance parameters. This computer is linked to a complex network of sensors and controllers throughout the car that monitor your car's operation and notify you at the first sign of

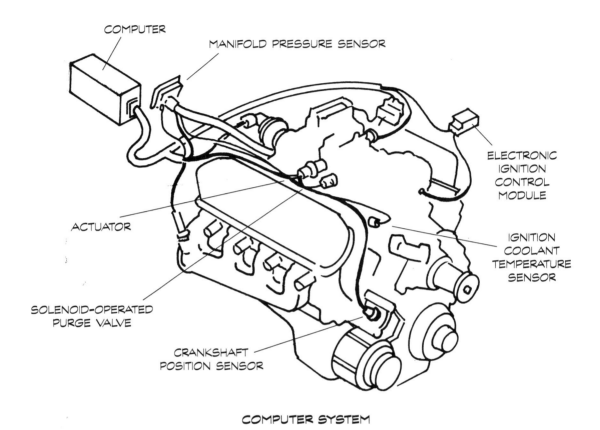

COMPUTER

MANIFOLD PRESSURE SENSOR

ELECTRONIC
IGNITION
CONTROL
MODULE

ACTUATOR

IGNITION
COOLANT
TEMPERATURE
SENSOR

SOLENOID-OPERATED
PURGE VALVE

CRANKSHAFT
POSITION SENSOR

COMPUTER SYSTEM

trouble. The OBD system notifies us of an operational malfunction by illuminating the "check engine" light on the dashboard.

When the "check engine" light comes on, your car's computer will generate an internal code identifying the root cause of the malfunction, which may range from something as simple as a loose gas cap to something as complex as an internal engine problem. The code, referred to as a "diagnostic trouble code" (DTC) will give a properly trained and equipped technician an idea of where to begin looking for the problem.

OBD systems monitor your vehicle's operation and performance to keep it running cleanly and efficiently. The OBD system can also give you advance warning to perform maintenance and help you avoid costly breakdowns. Additional controllers within the OBD system monitor key areas, including:

- Interior equipment and accessories
- Pollution controls
- Anti-lock braking systems
- Engine ignition
- Transmission function

The sections listed above are specifically designed to interact with each other. Each component in each section was also designed for a specific purpose on one specific car. Although some examples of this specialized interaction and design are very obvious, here are some examples of the "not-so-obvious":

- **The underhood section of a new car was designed with an air-dam that provides cooling airflow to the engine.**

  The air dam was damaged accidentally, but it didn't seem important enough to the owner to repair. Although the resulting failure was not immediately seen, over a period of several months the engine failed prematurely due to constant overheating. The cost to the car owner was a new engine.

- **A fairly new car repeatedly failed an emissions test.**

  The root cause of the failure turned out to be an improperly installed aftermarket accessory. The way the accessory was wired caused an abnormal imbalance in the car's electrical system. The electrical system, in turn, was working well beyond its designated parameters to accommodate the imbalance. This started a "domino effect" within the car's interactive systems, which led to an emissions failure.

■ **A damaged catalytic converter was replaced on another fairly new car.**

The replacement catalyst was not designed specifically for that car. Although the new catalyst worked for a short while, it wasn't long before the new catalyst was worn out. This caused a premature emissions failure that required an additional costly repair for the car owner.

An Ounce of Prevention is Worth a Pound of Cure...

P reventative maintenance is a lot easier on the pocketbook than major repairs. A well-maintained car will provide long and faithful service, and a well-maintained car will have a higher resale value as well. You will find a tear-out Auto Advisor Service and Safety Guide at the end of this introduction that will provide you with a handy place to record your car's maintenance and service for future reference. Always follow your manufacturer's suggested maintenance schedule, and be on the lookout for warning signs of upcoming trouble. Always put safety first.

Some of the key areas a car owner should monitor include:

Tires

Use a gauge to periodically check tire pressure, and remember to check your spare tire at the same time. Follow your manufacturer's instructions for proper inflation specifications. Also look for signs of tire damage or uneven wear, and always replace any questionable tires.

Lights

Frequently check your headlights (high-beam and low-beam), taillights, brake lights, turn signals, and four-way warning flashers for safe operation. When replacing headlights, also check the angle of the beam to assure safety for oncoming traffic.

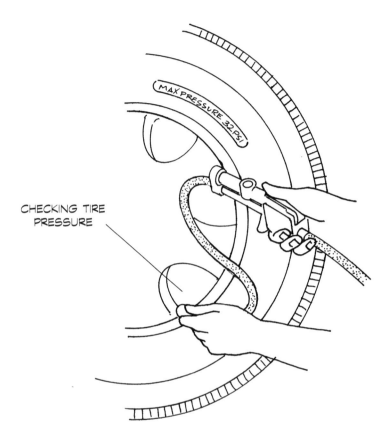

CHECKING TIRE
PRESSURE

MAX PRESSURE 32 PSI

Visibility

Always keep your windows and mirrors clean for proper visibility. Always keep washer fluid in your windshield washer tank, and change your windshield wipers when they first show signs of wear. In temperatures below freezing, make certain that your washer fluid will not freeze on your windshield. If you live in an urban area with high ozone levels you will need to change your windshield wipers more frequently due to the deteriorating effects of air pollution on rubber products.

"Check Engine" Light

Pay close attention to this light on your dashboard. If your "check engine" light does come on, it is usually safe to drive your car short distances until it can be serviced. If, however, the light is flashing, there is an unusual noise or smell, it is accompanied by another warning light or indicator, it is performing poorly, then park the car and seek immediate service.

Fuel Economy

An unexplained change in fuel economy is often one of the first indicators of a malfunction. Perform monthly fuel economy checks by recording your odometer reading before you fill up. When you fill up again, record the new odometer reading. Subtract the old odometer reading from the new reading, and divide that number by the amount of fuel it took to re-fill the tank. This is your "miles-per-gallon" (MPG) fuel economy rate. Note: Colder weather will normally cause a slight decrease in fuel economy.

Noises and smells

Always be on the lookout for new noises and smells, and have your technician check them out. Even the most seemingly insignificant things are worth further investigation to prevent a possible failure or a safety risk.

Performance and Handling

Pay close attention to changes in the way your car performs and handles. If you notice it is pulling to one side or another, you may have a low tire, an alignment problem, a steering system problem, a brake malfunction, or a handful of other possible causes. See your technician soon. And if you notice a change in performance, this is another indication that it is time to see your technician.

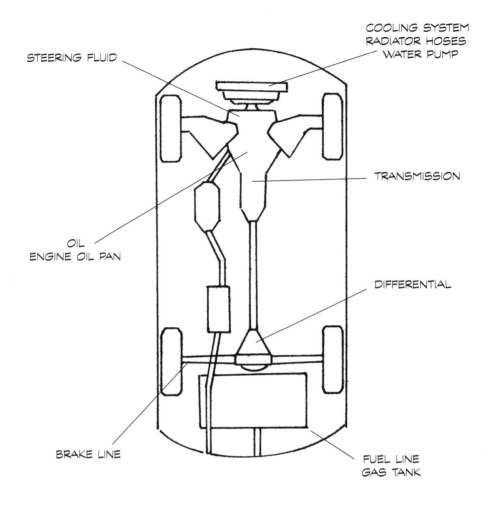

FLUID LEAKS IN A CAR

Leaks

For a car, leaks are one of the first signs of age. Be aware of any new spots on your driveway, and seek service soon to determine its origin. Fluid levels must be maintained to avoid major repairs and to keep your car running properly. If the leak is severe, do not start or drive the car; seek immediate service.

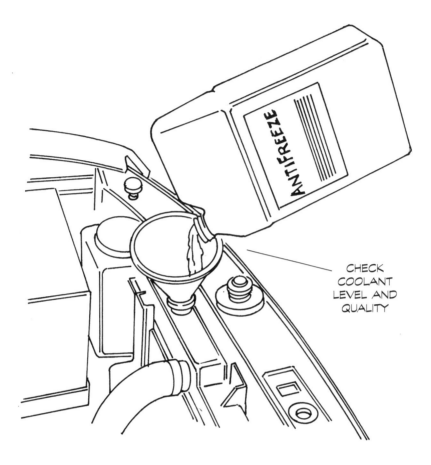

CHECK
COOLANT
LEVEL AND
QUALITY

When you bring your car to your technician for a "check-up," some of the additional areas your technician should check include:

- Oil level and quality
- Coolant level and quality
- Transmission fluid level and quality
- Brake fluid level and quality
- Power steering fluid level and quality
- Air filter
- PCV Valve

- Belts
- Hoses
- Suspension
- Drive axle boots
- Front end components (steering system)
- Battery
- Windshield washer fluid

When you are on the road, it's also a good idea to have the following safety equipment on board:

- Mobile phone
- Spare tire–make sure it is properly inflated
- Jack and heavy board (for a base)
- Lug wrench and key (if needed)
- Extra windshield washer fluid
- Jumper cables
- Flashlight–make sure it is in good working condition
- Spare flashlight batteries
- Warning signs or flares
- First aid kit
- Blanket
- Potable water (in hot climates)
- Emergency food supply
- Shovel and sand (in snowy climates)

Auto Advisor Service & Safety Guide

Some Helpful Information to Provide Your Technician

In addition to a written service and repair record, it will help your technician to know:

- What is the car doing specifically?
- Does it happen when the temperature is hot or cold?
- Does it happen on the first start of the day, or does it happen all day long?
- Does it happen at idle, at cruise, or at specific speeds?
- Is the "check engine" light on?
- When was the last time it was emission tested, and did it pass?
- When was the last time the car was worked on, and what was done to it?
- Does the car have any leaks, and what colors are they?
- Does the car overheat easily?
- Are there any problems with exterior lights (headlights, tail-lights, warning lights)?
- Are there any problems with interior lights (dash panel, courtesy lights)?
- Was an aftermarket (not original equipment) accessory recently installed?
- Are there any problems with electric windows or door locks?
- Do you hear noise when you brake or coast?
- Do you hear noise when you are in park, in gear, or in neutral?
- Do you hear noise at idle speeds, or at higher speeds?
- Do you hear noise when you turn a corner, or when you are going straight?
- As a courtesy to your technician, are there any special instructions they should have before they take your car for a test-drive?

CUT-OUT

Pre-trip Safety Checklist

In addition to a pre-trip "check-up" with a qualified technician, it is a good idea to have the following equipment on-board if you are planning a trip:

- Mobile phone
- Spare tire—make sure it is properly inflated
- Jack and heavy board (for a base)
- Lug wrench and wheel key (if needed)
- Windshield washer fluid
- Jumper cables
- Flashlight–make sure it is in good operating condition
- Spare flashlight batteries
- Warning signs or flares
- First aid kit
- Blanket
- Potable water (in hot climates)
- Shovel and sand (in snowy climates)

Your "Check Engine" Light

Pay close attention to this light on your dashboard. If your "check engine" light does come on, it is usually safe to continue your trip until it can be serviced unless:

- The light is flashing
- There is an unusual noise or smell
- It is accompanied by another warning light or indicator
- It is performing poorly

If any of these things occur, it is wise to park the car and seek immediate service.

MPG

Perform monthly fuel economy checks by recording your odometer reading before you fill up. When you fill up again, record the new odometer reading. Subtract the old odometer reading from the new reading, and divide that number by the amount of fuel it took to re-fill the tank. This is your "miles-per-gallon" (MPG) fuel economy rate. Record your monthly fuel economy in the chart below.

DATE	BEGINNING MILEAGE	ENDING MILEAGE	AMOUNT OF FUEL	MPG

Oil Change and Service Record

DATE	SERVICE/REPAIR COMPLETED	PARTS REPLACED	WHERE THE REPAIR WAS DONE

ABS. *See* ANTI-LOCK BRAKE SYSTEM.

AC. Recognized as an abbreviation used to mean ALTERNATING CURRENT in electrical work, this term is also used by automobile repair technicians to describe air conditioning.

Accelerator Pedal. The accelerator pedal is the elongated, vertical pedal that is located beneath the vehicle operator's right foot. The accelerator pedal determines the ENGINE speed and power output by controlling the position of the engine THROTTLE VALVE. The throttle valve controls the air flowing into the engine CYLINDERs.

Accelerator Pump. The accelerator pump is a small piston or diaphragm pump within a CARBURETOR. The pump operates via the gas pedal THROTTLE linkage. The throttle LINKAGE moves the pump piston or diaphragm when the driver depresses the ACCELERATOR PEDAL. As the pump moves, additional GAS

squirts into each engine CYLINDER. Therefore, at low engine speed, the accelerator pump momentarily enriches the air/fuel mixture.

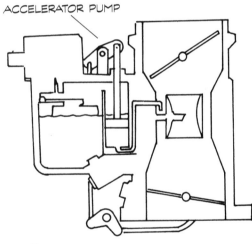

ACCELERATOR PUMP

CROSS-SECTION OF A CARBURETOR SHOWING AN ACCELERATOR PUMP

If the pump fails to work, a hesitation in vehicle acceleration often occurs. Failure may indicate that a repair or rebuild of the carburetor is necessary.

Accumulator. The accumulator is a chamber, sometimes containing a

SPRING and PISTON that stores pressure in an air or hydraulic system.

■ In an AIR CONDITIONING SYSTEM, an accumulator traps the REFRIGERANT flow for a short time, giving the refrigerant liquid an interval in which evaporation may occur. This unit helps prevent damage to the air conditioning COMPRESSOR, which cannot compress a liquid.

■ In an ANTILOCK BRAKE SYSTEM, the accumulator provides temporary storage of high-pressure BRAKE FLUID.

■ In an AUTOMATIC TRANSMISSION, the accumulator cushions the shock of hydraulic gear-shifting action. The accumulator absorbs and slows the build-up of clutch and brake band HYDRAULIC PRESSUREs. This action tailors the speed-matching character of TRANSMISSION gearing so smooth shifts occur.

If a transmission slips or chatters when shifting from one gear to another, the accumulator action may be suspect.

Advance. An advance is the moving ahead of engine ignition spark TIMING in relation to the engine PISTON action. In modern vehicles the advance is controlled by the engine computer. The computer tailors the amount of SPARK ADVANCE to maximize FUEL burning. An efficient fuel burn ensures good economy and power, while minimizing harmful EXHAUST EMISSIONS. For performance and EMISSION CONTROL reasons, the computerized ignition advance rate is not usually an adjustable item in the modern automobile IGNITION SYSTEM.

Aftercooler. *See* INTERCOOLER.

Air Bag. The air bag is a balloon-type passenger safety device that automatically inflates on vehicle impact. The air bag, sometimes termed as a PASSIVE RESTRAINT, is usually housed in the STEERING WHEEL, the dash, and/or door panels.

If triggered into action during a collision, a spent air bag must be serviced by a qualified and trained service technician.

Air Cleaner (ACL). An air cleaner is a filtering device, often termed the AIR FILTER, connected to the air intake system that removes dirt and dust from the engine air supply.

Since an engine gulps large amounts of air during operation, air cleaner replacement is an important part of normal vehicle maintenance.

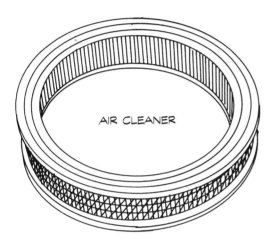

AIR CLEANER

Air Conditioning System (ACS or A/C). An air conditioning system is an accessory that modifies the air temperature and humidity before it enters the vehicle passenger compartment. An ACS can be classified as manual or automatic. Manual systems have settings in temperature, airflow, and BLOWER MOTOR speed determined by the operator through SWITCH settings. Automatic systems, more complex than manual systems, require only temperature and blower motor speed settings. The auto-matic system adjusts for needed system changes to maintain the set interior temperature.

Air Filter. *See* AIR CLEANER (ACL).

Airflow Control (Sensor). Used in some FUEL INJECTION systems, airflow control measures the amount of air mass entering the engine CYLINDERs. As the airflow is allowed into the engine by the driver-controlled THROTTLE PLATE, it is measured accurately by the air-flow meter. The fuel injection then adds the proper amount of FUEL. The unit is often called the MASS AIRFLOW SENSOR, VOLUME AIRFLOW SENSOR, or INTAKE AIR SENSOR.

Air/Fuel Ratio. The mixture proportions of air and FUEL supplied to the ENGINE is called the air/fuel ratio. In modern cars, the ratio is calculated and controlled by the engine computer. An average value (called STOICHIO-METRIC FUEL RATIO) is 14.7 parts air to one part fuel vapor. A rich mixture (about 12 to 1) supplies good engine starting, cold running, and high power. A lean mixture (about 17 to 1) provides an economical cruising mixture. If incorrect, a too rich or lean air/fuel ratio results in exhaust pollution, poor fuel economy, and engine performance loss.

Air/fuel ratio error may result from a dirty AIR FILTER, intake system air leaks, improper EMISSION CONTROL operations, or poor CARBURETOR or FUEL INJECTION calibration.

Air Injection System (AIS). An AIS is an EMISSION CONTROL system that injects low-pressure air into the engine EXHAUST SYSTEM. The injected air causes an afterburning of unused, leftover engine FUEL in the exhaust gases. This burning action lowers air pollution. Air injection is found in use in CATALYTIC CONVERTER equipped exhaust systems.

Air Spring. An air spring is a flexible bag filled with compressed air that is sometimes found in luxury vehicles. Taking the place of a vehicle's suspension COILs or LEAF springs in the SUSPENSION system, the air spring bags contract and expand as road bumps occur. The air ride system pressure may adjust to raise or lower the ride-height and level the vehicle as carrying weight changes.

ALDL (Assembly Line Data Link). A connection point that allows electronic communication with the vehicle computer.

All-Wheel Drive (AWD). A type of vehicle DRIVETRAIN that supplies power to all four wheels. AWD is often found in a vehicle that has no TWO-WHEEL DRIVE availability. AWD is primarily available for vehicles that operate on roads having poor traction conditions, but the vehicle has little or no recommended off-road capability.

Alternating Current (AC). Alternating current is an electric current that flows through a wiring CIRCUIT first in one direction and then in the other. Alternating current is not normally used in automotive circuits. However, an automotive ALTERNATOR produces AC that is changed to DIRECT CURRENT (DC) by a voltage rectifier.

Alternator. An alternator is an engine-driven device that converts mechanical energy into electric energy. The electricity produced by the alternator charges the BATTERY and supplies power for the vehicle's electrical equipment. An alternator is sometimes called the AC generator. An alternator is usually driven by an accessory belt or belts. DRIVE BELT tension is important to proper alternator output. Belts should be adjusted using a tension gauge.

Ammeter. An ammeter is a meter that measures the rate of current that flows through an electric CIRCUIT. Usually located in the vehicle's INSTRUMENT PANEL, the ammeter shows the driver the electrical charge going to or from the BATTERY.

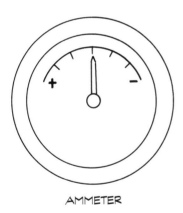

AMMETER

Ampere. An ampere is a unit of measurement for electric current. An ammeter may be calibrated according to the ampere delivery rate which can be delivered by the vehicle ALTERNATOR. *Also see* VOLT *and* OHM.

Ampere-Hour Capacity. Ampere-hour capacity battery ratings are based on the electric current that a BATTERY can deliver for 20 hours. The high ampere-hour capacity rated battery has greater ENGINE cranking power over a longer period of time than a lower rated battery.

Analog Gauge. An analog gauge indicates a measured amount with a pointer or needle upon a scale. For example, most gas gauges are analog.

ANALOG GAUGE

Antifreeze. Antifreeze is a chemical mixture added to the engine COOLANT to prevent freezing. The antifreeze lowers the freezing temperature and increases the boiling point of the engine coolant. During replacement, car manufacturers recommend specific antifreeze or coolant mixture percentages. The percentage needed relies upon the expected vehicle operating climate and performance conditions. Various antifreeze chemicals are available and each has its own characteristics and limitations.

Check with a qualified vehicle service technician for antifreeze service replacement recommendations.

Anti-lock Brake System (ABS). An anti-lock brake system is designed to help prevent WHEEL lockup and skid during vehicle stops. Preventing wheel lock helps to retain vehicle steering control during emergency braking. The ABS system senses the speed of the wheels electronically and computes the amount of braking pressure that is needed to slow or stop the vehicle without a loss of TIRE traction. The ABS may control the braking rate of all four wheels or just two rear wheels, depending on the vehicle's brake system design.

Arcing. Arcing is an electric spark that jumps an air GAP between two electric conductors, such as wires or electric contacts. Problem arcing can occur between CIRCUITS, as from one SPARK PLUG wire to another.

Arcing may damage equipment operation and interfere with computers and radios.

Armature. An armature is a part containing iron which rotates within a magnetic field. The armature is used in electric motors and generators. In a STARTER MOTOR, the armature rotates to move a mechanical part. In an ALTERNATOR or GENERATOR, the armature spins through a magnetic field. The magnetic field produces electric current.

Armatures may become damaged if unit bearings wear excessively, or if electric current, loads, and unit temperatures get too high.

Aspect Ratio. The ratio of profile in comparing TIRE height to width is called the aspect ratio. Carefully calculated by vehicle designers for good handling characteristics, the aspect ratio should remain the same when tires are replaced.

Automatic Choke. The automatic choke is a device used in a CARBURETOR to restrict air flow. The CHOKE enriches the FUEL mixture for cold ENGINE starts and operation during warm-up. When cold, the fuel vaporizes for burning at a very slow rate, so more fuel (a rich mixture) is added for mixture compensation.

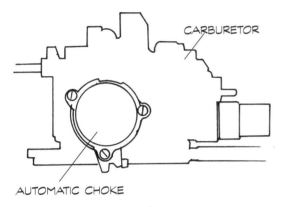

CARBURETOR

AUTOMATIC CHOKE

Automatic Headlight Dimmer. An automatic headlight dimmer is a photo sensor that detects light, and automatically selects the proper HEADLIGHT function to high- or low-beam for the driving conditions.

Automatic Level Control. An automatic level control is a SUSPENSION system that compensates for variations in vehicle load by maintaining the body at a predetermined height. Leveling systems usually contain ride height sensors, an air pump and its hoses, and suspension system air springs. *Also see* AIR SPRING.

Automatic Transmission. An automatic transmission is a unit that automatically changes GEAR RATIOS. The automatic transmission selects the ratio depending on road speed and ENGINE power available, instead of the driver shifting by hand as a MANUAL TRANSMISSION requires. While some vehicles require changing of automatic transmission fluid and the transmission FILTER during the operational life of the vehicle, others do not. Some TRANSMISSIONS require adjustment of internal BAND clearances or linkages.

Always check with the vehicle manufacturer or a qualified service technician for automatic transmission service recommendations.

AWD. *See* ALL-WHEEL DRIVE.

Axle. The axle is a supporting crossbar or tube upon which the vehicle wheels

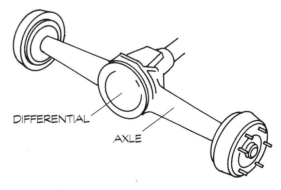

DIFFERENTIAL

AXLE

rotate. An axle supports the vehicle through the attached SUSPENSION springs. The axle may also supply the drive TORQUE to a WHEEL.

Axle Ratio. Often called the DIFFERENTIAL ratio, an axle ratio is the drive speed ratio between the rotational speed of the input shaft or DRIVESHAFT, and the speed of the rotating output shaft or AXLE SHAFT. The GEAR RATIO determines the power transfer and speed available to the vehicle drive wheels.

Axle Shaft. An axle shaft is a metal shaft that connects the DIFFERENTIAL drive gear assembly to the driving wheels. The shaft is supported by BEARINGs. Some shafts contain joints that allow angled operation during suspension travel or vehicle steering.

Axle shafts in most vehicles require little or no attention, unless DRIVELINE joints require service or replacement. Consult with a qualified technician for AXLE SHAFT service.

Backfire. Backfire is an unusual banging or popping noise heard from beneath the hood or the vehicle. Normally caused by a malfunction, backfire usually occurs when the driver depresses the ACCELERATOR PEDAL, releases the accelerator pedal, or drives uphill. The noise may originate from the engine air intake or exhaust system. Backfire may be caused by FUEL system troubles, IGNITION misfire or ENGINE VALVE malfunction.

Backfire occurrences indicate that immediate attention should be paid to the engine condition, fuel delivery and IGNITION SYSTEM tuning.

Backlash. Backlash is a term used for clearances built into gear drives. In gear drives, a slight amount of backlash CLEARANCE is normal between the moving parts. The backlash allows for lubrication and heat expansion clearances. Insufficient backlash may cause the GEARS to generate too much heat under a load. However, excessive backlash can cause undue gear tooth clearances, called PLAY, and produce DRIVELINE clanking noises.

Balljoint. A balljoint is a ball-and-socket mechanical joint that allows tilting or rotation of connected parts. The balljoint consists of a metal ball and its protruding threaded stud, and the balljoint body. The stud goes through a tapered hole and is seated to the mating part—usually the STEERING KNUCKLE—by the attaching nut tightness.

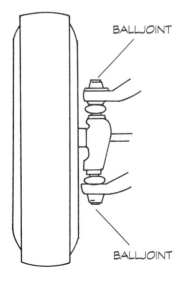

BALLJOINT

BALLJOINT

The ball rides within a lubricated metal socket. The balljoint socket assembly is either pressed or attached with metal bolts to the adjoining part, normally a suspension CONTROL ARM.

In steering applications, the balljoint receives high loads, so the balljoint always needs adequate lubrication. You may also find balljoints used in some internal ENGINE VALVE operations or mechanical LINKAGEs, such as in the ball-and-fulcrum ROCKER ARM.

Band. Used in an AUTOMATIC TRANSMISSION, the band is a metal COIL or wrap that is lined internally with FRICTION material. The band surrounds a metal drum. When applied using HYDRAULIC oil pressure and a PISTON, the band clamps tightly around the drum and halts drum rotation. The drum connects to gears within the PLANETARY GEARset of the TRANSMISSION. If the band fails because of friction lining wear, poor adjustment, or low hydraulic apply pressure, the transmission slips. The ENGINE will overspeed and the vehicle will fail to accelerate or will not be able to move at all. A slipping band overheats, and eventually, the band friction lining prematurely wears and burns.

Older cars with adjustable bands should have regular transmission maintenance, including band adjustment.

Barometric Pressure Sensor (BARO). The barometric pressure sensor detects changes in engine operating altitude. Detection of altitude air pressure changes becomes necessary for close control of the air/fuel mixture. As altitude increases, OXYGEN content changes per cubic foot of air volume. A FUEL INJECTION system adjusts for this natural environment change. In some applications, the BARO sensor is built into the MANIFOLD ABSOLUTE PRESSURE (MAP) SENSOR.

Battery. An electrical storage unit used in the automobile, the battery is a wet-cell chemical device. It chemically stores power that it receives from the engine ALTERNATOR or GENERATOR. A vehicle battery contains a DIRECT CURRENT (DC) polarity. The electricity potential is stored in a wet ELECTROLYTE acid chemical. The battery PLATE chemical reactions release the electrical power for cranking the engine. The battery also powers vehicle electrical components.

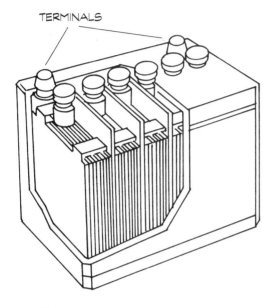

TERMINALS

Cᴜᴛᴀᴡᴀʏ ᴏꜰ ʙᴀᴛᴛᴇʀʏ sʜᴏᴡɪɴɢ
ᴄᴇʟʟs ᴀɴᴅ ᴘʟᴀᴛᴇs

Corrosion on battery terminals can cause many different problems, including poor starting. Battery terminals should be cleaned on a regular basis.

The wet-cell battery contains liquid ELECTROLYTE acid and lead PLATEs. The acid and lead can cause personal injury. The battery should only be serviced by knowledgeable and qualified persons. *See* BATTERY ACID.

Battery Acid. The liquid used in a BATTERY is called battery acid. The acid or ELECTROLYTE is a mixture of SULFURIC ACID and water that reacts with lead PLATEs to store and release electricity.

Battery acids are to be handled with extreme caution. Chemical burns may result from contact. Especially guard physically sensitive areas, such as eyes, if you work around the wet-cell battery. If acid exposure contacts eyes or sensitive areas, immediate medical attention is recommended. Do not touch the acid or acid residue build-up on battery terminals. Also, clothing may be damaged by battery acid.

BCM. *See* BODY CONTROL MODULE.

BDC. *See* BOTTOM DEAD CENTER.

Bead. The bead is a portion of the TIRE that seals against the metal WHEEL. The circular bead is shaped to fit the outer circumference of a wheel rim and seal tightly when the tire is properly pressurized. A tire's bead is first constructed with internal steel wires. These are wrapped and reinforced by wire belts, rubber layers, and PLIES of the tire.

Bearing. A bearing is a material which transmits mechanical energy from one part to another without excess wear. Made of wear-resistant materials, bearings must receive adequate lubrication. A bearing absorbs FRICTION heat created between moving parts. Usually a sliding insert material, ball, or roller device, a bearing is normally replaced if it fails from fatigue or loses lubrication. *See* BUSHING.

Bendix. *See* OVER-RUNNING CLUTCH.

Bleeding. Bleeding is a work process that removes air from a HYDRAULIC circuit. Bleeding frees air from the brake, cooling, fuel, or power steering circuits. A hydraulic circuit with air in the fluid circuit will not function correctly. Air compresses, whereas fluid will not. Usually done by opening a bleed valve or hose while pressure operating the system, bleeding allows the air to escape. Hydraulic fluid always needs to be replenished to replace the air expelled.

Blowby. Combustion gases that leak from cylinder COMBUSTION past the ENGINE PISTON RINGS are called blowby. Usually a sign of high engine CYLINDER wear or damage, blowby usually enters the engine oil reservoir or CRANKCASE. Blowby, therefore, often shows up as

vented, oil-laden vapor exiting to the air intake system via the POSITIVE CRANKCASE VENTILATION (PCV) **valve.**

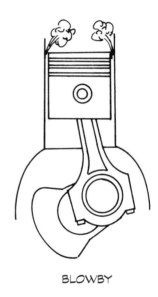

BLOWBY

Engines having excess blowby are candidates for major repair or overhaul.

Blower. *See* SUPERCHARGER.

Blower Motor. An electric motor that moves air through air conditioning and heater ducts. The blower motor spins a squirrel cage type fan to draw air and push the temperature-conditioned air into the vehicle interior.

Body Control Module (BCM). The

body control module (BCM) is a computer that controls vehicle body and accessory systems. Operating in concert with other computers such as the POWERTRAIN CONTROL MODULE (PCM), the BCM monitors and governs the operation of items such as air conditioning, power accessories, and body system diagnostics.

Boost. Boost is a pressure that develops in the engine INTAKE MANIFOLD when a SUPERCHARGER or TURBOCHARGER operates. Using boost pressure, the supercharger or turbocharger enhances engine COMPRESSION and COMBUSTION pressures for increased vehicle acceleration. Boost pressure is closely controlled by a WASTEGATE to prevent engine damage.

Booster. A booster is a vacuum storage chamber, which assists the application of the vehicle BRAKEs. The ENGINE supplies the unit with engine MANIFOLD VACUUM through a one-way check valve. A METERING VALVE within the unit controls the amount of assist given to a BRAKE PEDAL application. The metering valve operates when the brake pedal is depressed by the driver.

Bottom Dead Center (BDC). A rotational position of the engine crankshaft. BDC occurs as the CONNECTING ROD and cylinder PISTON reach their lowest travel in the CYLINDER. Expressed in degrees of crankshaft rotation around the crankshaft center or MAIN BEARING, BDC occurs at 180 degrees when the cylinder volume reaches its maximum. *See* TOP DEAD CENTER and CRANKSHAFT.

Brake. A brake is an energy conversion device used to slow, stop, or hold an object. In an automobile, the brake applies at the WHEEL to stop or slow the vehicle. The brake converts vehicle momentum to frictional heat. To say the vehicle "needs brakes" indicates that the brake friction lining that causes halting of a spinning wheel has worn beyond its useful service life. The brake may be of drum or disc design.

Whether drum or disc design, the replacement of BRAKE LININGS should be accompanied with necessary servicing of the BRAKE DRUM, BRAKE DISC, and the HYDRAULIC BRAKE parts.

Brake Disc. A brake disc is a flat, circular frictional surface that rotates with the spinning vehicle WHEEL. When the brakes are applied, the disc receives abrasive force from the brake disc FRICTION pads. This action slows or stops wheel rotation. Brake discs need resurfacing or replacement if friction pads cause improper disc wear, metal scoring, or heat warping. A brake disc is often referred to as a brake ROTOR.

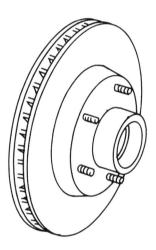

BRAKE DISC

Brake Drum. A metal drum that mounts inside a vehicle WHEEL and receives frictional stopping efforts is called the brake drum. The drum forms the outer rotating shell of a drum-style BRAKE. When applied by HYDRAULIC PRESSURE, the BRAKE LINING housed within the brake assembly presses outward

against the drum. Contact FRICTION between the brake material and the drum circumference slows or stops the drum. This action slows or stops the wheel rotation. Drum brakes are commonly found on the rear wheels of a vehicle. DRUM BRAKE designs are subject to low BRAKE PEDAL complaints due to excessive lining clearances or air contained in the BRAKE FLUID circuit. While most modern vehicles contain automatic brake adjusters, these can seize and halt their action and cause low brake pedal position.

A low or spongy-feeling brake pedal application should always be investigated by a qualified technician.

Brake Fade. Brake fade is caused by a pressure build-up of gasses between the BRAKE LINING and the BRAKE DRUM. The gasses are formed as the solvents that were used to bond the brake lining to the brake shoe are heated. Drum brake linings, contained within the enclosed brake drum, are subject to overheating and fade more frequently than DISC BRAKEs. Disc brakes are exposed to air circulation. Disc brakes, therefore, suffer less from overheating and fade.

Brake Fluid. Brake fluid is a hydraulic fluid used to operate HYDRAULIC BRAKE systems. The fluid transmits applied BRAKE PEDAL force and motion from the MASTER CYLINDER through the brakes' lines or tubing. Brake fluids are rated for the vehicle weight and heat loads.

 Brake fluids are hygroscopic, meaning they attract moisture, therefore they should not be stored in an open container. If it becomes necessary to add fluid to a master cylinder reservoir, always check with the car maker's recommendations for the fluid type needed.

Brake Horsepower. Brake horsepower is the power available from the engine CRANKSHAFT to do the work of moving the vehicle and operating accessory equipment.

Brake Light. A brake light is located at the rear of the vehicle, paired with a mating brake light on the vehicle's opposite side. The brake light lens is red in color. When illuminated, the light indicates that the vehicle service brakes are applied. The brake light is also referred to as a STOP LIGHT. The brake light usually operates from a BRAKE PEDAL switch located on the brake pedal LINKAGE or the MASTER CYLINDER.

Brake Lines. The brake lines are metal tubes and rubber hoses that connect the hydraulic MASTER CYLINDER to the hydraulic wheel CYLINDERs or CALIPERs in a BRAKE system. Since the rubber hoses are subject to flex from chassis SUSPENSION motion, WHEEL motion, or vehicle turning, these should be inspected each time a BRAKE LINING replacement is done.

Brake Lining. Brake lining is a friction-absorbing material attached to the BRAKE shoe or pad by rivets or a bonding process. The lining converts mechanical energy to heat energy to stop the vehicle when the brake linings press against the BRAKE DRUM or brake ROTOR. Brake linings are high-wear items, having a service life according to the quality of the lining and the use of the vehicle.

 Brake lining should be checked at least every 12,000 miles of vehicle use, and replaced by a qualified brake service technician as needed.

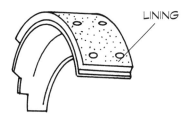

LINING

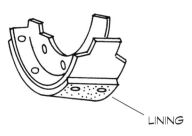

LINING

Brake Pedal. The brake pedal is a driver's foot-operated pedal normally located to the left of the ACCELERATOR PEDAL. Via an attached plunger rod, it operates the apply pistons of the braking system's MASTER CYLINDER. In turn, the master cylinder applies HYDRAULIC brake pressure to the vehicle brake circuits. The master cylinder does this proportionally in response to foot force upon the pedal. Therefore, the brake pedal controls the force of BRAKE LINING application to the rotating BRAKE DRUMS

or BRAKE DISCS at the vehicle wheels. The brake pedal force is sometimes assisted or boosted by a VACUUM or hydraulic pump. This power brake assist, therefore, lowers the energy requirement needed by the driver to slow or stop the vehicle.

Brake Pedal Position Sensor (PP or BPP). The brake pedal position sensor detects the driver's application of the BRAKE PEDAL. The information is sent to units such as the POWERTRAIN CONTROL MODULE and other CIRCUITs that adjust actuators in relation to the input information.

Breaker Point Ignition. A breaker point ignition system contains an electrical switch, or a set of switches, that operate current flow through the primary winding of the IGNITION COIL. Normally located within the IGNITION DISTRIBUTOR, the points turn the coil primary CIRCUIT on and off. Therefore, the points control the coil's secondary circuit firing. The coil's high voltage charges fires through the IGNITION SYSTEM to the SPARK PLUGS. Because of point tendency toward ARCING, point contact pitting, and point wear, the breaker point ignition system has been super-seded in late model vehicles by com-puterized coil operation.

Brush. A brush is a block of conducting material, such as CARBON, which trans-fers electric current between a non-moving part and a moving part. The brush rides against a rotating metal ring or JOURNAL called a COMMUTATOR to form a continuous electric CIRCUIT. The brush contact surface is usually made of a material known for high electrical conductivity, such as copper.

BTDC. An abbreviation meaning "before top dead center." The abbrevia-tion indicates any position of the CRANK-SHAFT swing between the crank-pin JOURNAL at 90 degrees before top dead center (TDC) on the upward stroke of the piston, and TDC. A typical SPARK PLUG firing time is slightly BTDC, before the crankshaft and PISTON reach TDC. *See* TOP DEAD CENTER.

Bushing. A bushing is a sleeve placed in a bore to serve as a bearing surface. In an ENGINE, TRANSMISSION, or other DRIVE-TRAIN component, the bushing is usually made of a soft metal substance, such as copper, bronze, aluminum, or babbitt alloy. Bushings in vehicle SUS-PENSION may be made of rubber or plas-tic. Rubber bushings usually need no lubrication. *Also see* BEARING.

Cable. A cable is a stranded wire, often covered with insulating material. Cables often connect components to transfer mechanical action, such as the cable that may connect a gas pedal to an engine THROTTLE PLATE. Some cables are insulated because they carry electrical current, such as a battery cable. If a cable carries electricity, a replacement cable must be the same size in length and diameter as its predecessor.

Please note that battery cables and their terminals receive attack from the acidic fumes given off from the BATTERY charging action. These cables should be regularly serviced to remove corrosion and acid build-up. The effects of build-up could interfere with a low-resistance cable connection.

Extreme care must be used in cleaning battery cable terminals to prevent personal contact with BATTERY ACID. Personal injury to exposed skin, especially the eyes, may occur. If cleaning is done, use only cleaning agents recommended for battery terminal service. Removal of cables normally requires disconnecting the NEGATIVE terminal first to prevent sparking. Sparking could ignite the HYDROGEN gases that are normally emitted from a charging battery wet cell.

Also, note that a loss of stored electronic memory can occur during battery CIRCUIT disconnection. In some electronic control systems, the computers may need to "relearn" certain parameters. In addition, certain items such as digital clocks may need resetting.

Caliper. Used in a DISC BRAKE, a caliper houses hydraulic PISTONS and brake pads. Connected by a hydraulic hose to the brake hydraulic system, the caliper responds to applied brake pressures by applying the BRAKE LINING to the BRAKE DISC. The action will slow or stop the spinning brake disc or ROTOR, and the WHEEL assembly.

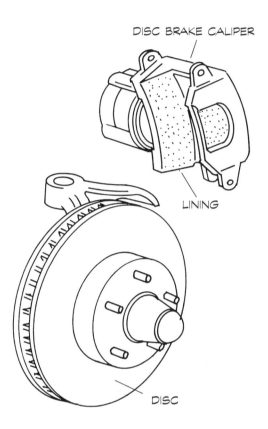

DISC BRAKE CALIPER

LINING

DISC

Cam. A cam is a rotating eccentric shape that converts rotary motion to linear, reciprocating motion. In ENGINEs, for example, the cam shape is used to form the lobes of the CAMSHAFT. The camshaft, often simply called the cam by auto repair technicians, is used with VALVE LIFTERS, FOLLOWERS, tappets and other VALVETRAIN components to open and close an engine's INTAKE VALVE and EXHAUST VALVE. A cam can also be used to operate mechanical FUEL injectors,

TRANSMISSION parts, air conditioner components, and many other mechanical objects.

Camber. The tilt of a wheel from the true vertical is called camber. Used in WHEEL ALIGNMENT, proper camber settings contribute to good vehicle handling and long TIRE wear. In degrees, if WHEEL tilt lies outward from the vehicle center at the top, the camber is termed as positive. If inward, camber is negative. Normally, camber is set to less than 1 degree, either negative or positive, in most vehicles. Differences in setting specifications side-to-side, of approximately ¼ to ½ degree, may be normal. Occasionally the left wheel, closest to the center of the road, is set slightly to a more positive camber than the right. This setting normally compensates for the crown of the roadway.

Cam Lobe. The cam lobe is the raised portion of the eccentrically-shaped base CAM circle.

Camshaft. The camshaft is housed within the ENGINE. It contains a series of CAM LOBES. The camshaft, often called the CAM, operates the ENGINE VALVES. A cam is driven by either GEARs and a TIM-ING CHAIN, or sprockets and a toothed belt. In a FOUR-CYCLE engine, such as that used in the automobile, the cam travels at half the rotating speed of the CRANKSHAFT. Camshafts are particularly prone to high wear due to inadequate or dirty lubricating oil.

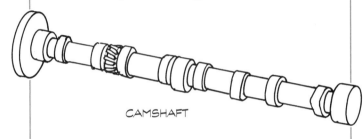

CAMSHAFT

Camshaft Position Sensor (CMP). A camshaft position sensor is a magnetic sensor or switch that provides the electronic engine computer with a signal voltage. The signal tells the position of the CAMSHAFT and ENGINE VALVEs.

Carbon (C). Carbon is a black, fluffy deposit left after the HYDROGEN burns from the GASOLINE or DIESEL FUEL. Left on engine parts such as PISTONs, PISTON RINGs, and VALVEs by the COMBUSTION, carbon acts as an abrasive on engine parts. If excess carbon builds from running a too rich FUEL mixture or prolonged slow-speed driving, high engine

heat cakes and hardens the carbon into an abrasive deposit. Engine life can be seriously reduced by these carbon deposits.

Carbon can also take up space in the COMBUSTION CHAMBER, thus raising the combustion ratio beyond the point that gasoline additives may prevent PRE-IGNITION. As well, glowing carbon deposits may pre-ignite fuel in the chamber and cause high-performance engine KNOCK. Carbon deposits may often be loosened by fuel system additives designed for this purpose. However, some additives are not recommended for use with a CATALYTIC CONVERTER. As well, some carbon particles may loosen, only to lodge beneath the VALVE SEAT. This action prevents proper VALVE seating and valve cooling. This results in CYLINDER malfunction from COMPRESSION loss, usually requiring major repair.

The best cure is PREVENTIVE MAINTENANCE. Proper and timely tune-ups, quality fuel, coupled with occasional passing gear or highway driving to blow carbon fluff from the combustion chambers, does a lot toward eliminating carbon deposit troubles.

Carbon Dioxide (CO_2). Carbon dioxide is an odorless, colorless gas that is produced as HYDROCARBONS burn. In automobiles, CO_2 is one of several gases resulting from COMBUSTION. In a properly tuned engine, CO_2 tests high in the engine exhaust. In nature, CO_2 is consumed by vegetation and OXYGEN (O) is produced.

Carbon Monoxide (CO). Odorless, colorless, and poisonous, carbon monoxide is a GAS that results from incomplete COMBUSTION. CO is a pollutant in engine exhaust gases that climbs in volume to unacceptable levels should engine combustion be improper.

Carburetor (Carb). The carburetor is an engine fuel system unit that mixes air and FUEL. When correctly calibrated, the carburetor emits proper air/fuel mixtures for engine starting, idle, economy, power, and clean EXHAUST EMISSIONS.

Receiving air from the AIR CLEANER's filter, and fuel from the FUEL TANK through a FILTER and pump, the carburetor supplies a COMBUSTIBLE MIXTURE to the engine INTAKE MANIFOLD. The carburetor does so by piping air and fuel through internal circuits or devices that include the CHOKE, float, idle circuit, accelerator pump, low-speed circuit, high-speed circuit, and power circuit.

A carburetor that fails to meet performance or emissions standards in any of its functions or circuits may be repaired, rebuilt, or replaced. Because of its complexity, however, this unit is usually serviced by a qualified technician, or by a rebuilding and remanufacturing center.

Caster. Caster is the tilting of the front suspension steering pin or axis forward or backward. Positive caster tilts the axis rearward at the top. Positive caster provides directional steering stability. Negative caster tilts the axis forward at the top, which provides ease of steering when turning. Most vehicles are set about 1 to 2 degrees plus or minus of true vertical (0 degrees), with little difference in setting from side-to-side. If differences exist in desired specifications, they usually provide the necessary climb in steering to offset the natural CAMBER built into two-lane highways.

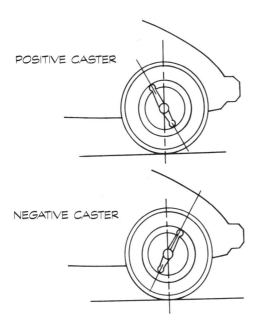

POSITIVE CASTER

NEGATIVE CASTER

Catalyst. A material that causes a chemical reaction without participating in the process is called a catalyst. For example, the catalyst in the CATALYTIC CONVERTER causes chemical changes that lessen air pollution. But the catalyst does not diminish or participate in the reaction process. A catalyst's abilities, however, can be lessened by coating the catalyst surfaces with foreign materials, such as an engine's COOLANT or OIL. Catalytic converters can also be damaged by improper AIR/FUEL RATIOS.

Catalytic Converter. A catalytic converter is a chamber in a vehicle's engine EXHAUST SYSTEM that houses the CATALYST. The converter reduces the levels of HYDROCARBONS, CARBON MONOXIDE and NITROGEN OXIDES emitted into the atmosphere. Vehicle malfunctions can overcome its beneficial effects. For example, if a vehicle runs too rich for an extended period, the catalyst becomes flooded with unburned hydrocarbons and carbon monoxide. The unit becomes overworked and overheated as it burns the pollution. A FUEL mixture may become too lean, with insufficient fuel content to support complete COMBUSTION. The combustion fire goes out before the fuel completely burns. Unburned exhaust hydrocarbon content will rise. Often the smell of SULFURIC OXIDES, similar to the smell of rotten eggs, emits from the EXHAUST PIPE as an overheated catalyst operates hard to clean up the effects of an improper mixture.

The effectiveness of a catalyst can be checked by exhaust gas analysis. The vehicle exhaust is tested, or sniffed, by a test instrument that checks the exhaust pipe flow for excessive pollution. Two types of modern catalytic converters exist: the three-way converter, and the three-way with oxidation catalytic converter.

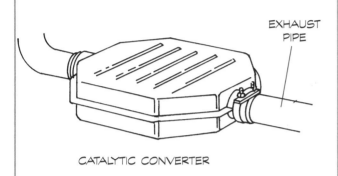

EXHAUST PIPE

CATALYTIC CONVERTER

If a converter becomes deficient in cleansing ability, caused predominately by leaded GASOLINE or COOLANT contaminated combustion, a catalytic converter is serviced or replaced.

Center Differential. A center differential is located between the two drive AXLES and TRANSMISSION of some FOUR-WHEEL DRIVE (4WD) or ALL-WHEEL DRIVE (AWD) vehicles. When unlocked, the unit allows differing DRIVESHAFT speeds to the vehicle's front and rear. The center differential is also called INTERAXLE DIFFERENTIAL.

Central Fuel Injection (CFI). *See* THROTTLE BODY FUEL INJECTION.

Centrifugal Advance. The centrifugal advance is a mechanism in an IGNITION DISTRIBUTOR containing rotating flyweights. The advance alters SPARK IGNITION TIMING by using centrifugal force exerted on the weights. The faster the ENGINE operates, the farther outward the distributor weights spin. The action mechanically causes an ignition SPARK ADVANCE. The spark must occur sooner to provide adequate air/fuel mixture burning time. In late-model vehicles, the DISTRIBUTOR centrifugal advance unit is replaced by computer control.

Cetane Number. Cetane is a reference measure of the ignition quality in DIESEL FUEL. The lower the cetane number, the higher the temperature required to ignite a diesel fuel. Cetane also measures the speed of fuel burning. Most automobile DIESEL ENGINEs require No. 1 cetane rated FUEL.

Charcoal Canister. The charcoal canister is a can containing activated charcoal. The canister traps GASOLINE vapors emitted from the fuel system when the ENGINE is off. When the engine operates, vapors purge from the canister to the air intake system and are consumed in the engine COMBUSTION. The charcoal canister is often referred to as the PURGE CANISTER.

Charge Light. The charge light is an INSTRUMENT PANEL light that illuminates to indicate the BATTERY is not charging. The charge light may be replaced by an AMMETER in some vehicles.

Charging Rate. Charging rate is the electrical AMPERE flow from the ALTERNATOR into the BATTERY. The charging rate average must exceed current draw or the battery will become depleted.

Chassis. The chassis describes the strong supporting platform of a body-over-frame style vehicle. The chassis consists of the vehicle FRAME. The chassis houses the DRIVETRAIN components, and SUSPENSION and STEERING components. In unibody design vehicles, the chassis is integrally built into the body structure of the vehicle. The unibody chassis, therefore consists of various body parts that are made of high-strength steel (HSS) for structural integrity, strength, and controlled-force flow during vehicle collision. *See* UNIBODY.

Check Valve. The check valve opens to admit the passage of air or fluid only in one direction, halting the reverse flow to prevent undesirable action.

Chip. The chip is a tiny integrated electronic CIRCUIT capable of performing many electrical functions and calculations. A computer chip may be replaceable, reprogrammable, or soldered to a circuit board, depending on the computer design.

Choke. Used in the CARBURETOR, the choke is a device that blocks intake air and therefore enriches the FUEL mixture available to the engine CYLINDERs. In modern vehicles, the choke usually operates automatically when starting a cold ENGINE. Choke failure may cause hard engine starting, stalling, inadequate fast IDLE SPEED, or poor FUEL economy.

If a vehicle is carbureted, the choke should be serviced with choke cleaner and lubricant during an engine TUNE-UP, to ensure proper mechanical choke action.

Circuit. A circuit is a complete path for electric current, air, or fluid flow, including the circuit power source.

Circuit Breaker. A circuit breaker is a resettable protective electrical device. The breaker opens an electric CIRCUIT to prevent operational heat damage when the circuit overloads. *Also see* FUSE.

Clearance. Clearance is space designed between two moving parts, or between a moving and a stationary part. For example, a BEARING clearance fills with lubricating OIL or grease when the mechanism runs. The lubrication thus prevents FRICTION heat, wear and seizing. If excess clearance exists between such parts, rattling or knocking noises may occur.

Closed Loop. Closed loop is an engine operating condition where the AIR/FUEL RATIO is closely controlled by the POWERTRAIN CONTROL MODULE (PCM). The air/fuel ratio varies between slightly rich to slightly lean. Proper CATALYTIC CONVERTER operation requires closed-loop fuel control. OXYGEN SENSORs in the EXHAUST SYSTEM inform the PCM of current air/fuel conditions and the PCM varies the air/fuel ratio accordingly.

Failures in EMISSION CONTROLs and ENGINE performance should be immediately investigated.

Clutch. The clutch is a coupling that connects and disconnects a shaft and its driving power. In an automotive DRIVETRAIN, the clutch engages and disengages engine power to the TRANSMISSION. In air conditioning, the clutch engages and disengages the belt-driven pulley at the COMPRESSOR shaft. If defective, a clutch can slip, fail to apply or release, or chatter during engagement.

To ensure proper operation and long friction lining life, DRIVELINE clutch linkages are usually adjusted so that approximately one inch of free PLAY occurs at the CLUTCH PEDAL before the clutch begins disengagement. The intervals for adjustment depend on the manufacturer recommendations and the type of vehicle use. Urban or heavy-duty use often demands more frequent adjustment intervals.

Clutch Disc. The clutch disc is a circular PLATE that rides splined upon the manual transmission INPUT SHAFT. Located between the clutch PRESSURE PLATE and the engine FLYWHEEL, the clutch disc contains FRICTION lining on both sides of the disc. When the lining is squeezed by clutch application,

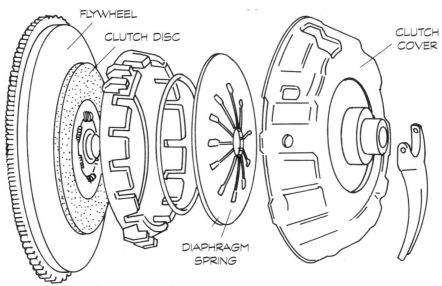

FLYWHEEL

CLUTCH DISC

CLUTCH COVER

DIAPHRAGM SPRING

EXPLODED VIEW OF A CLUTCH MECHANISM

caused by the driver's release of the CLUTCH PEDAL, the engine's TORQUE is transmitted from the flywheel. The torque flows through the clutch disc to the input shaft of the TRANSMISSION.

Failures of the clutch disc lining, or lining contamination can cause CLUTCH slippage and engagement chatter. Also, failures of the disc's torsional cushioning SPRINGs can cause clutch chatter during engagement.

Clutch Engage Switch (CES). The clutch engage switch is an electric switch located on the clutch LINKAGE to indicate the CLUTCH action to a computer.

Clutch Pedal. A clutch pedal is operated by the driver's foot. The driver depresses the clutch pedal to move LINKAGE and disconnect the engine power from the TRANSMISSION.

Periodic clutch pedal linkage adjustments are usually necessary to maintain CLUTCH service life.

Clutch Shaft. The clutch shaft is the INPUT SHAFT of a MANUAL TRANSMISSION. An engine-driven clutch housing rotates the clutch plate. When the CLUTCH is engaged, the housing and its plate drives the TRANSMISSION clutch shaft through the CLUTCH DISC. The friction-material-lined clutch disc is squeezed between the clutch plate and the FLY-WHEEL surface. The clutch disc center SPLINE thereby transfers engine power to the transmission input shaft.

Coil. Used in the engine IGNITION SYSTEM, the coil is a voltage transformer. The coil raises BATTERY voltage to the high voltage required to fire the ignition system. When the coil is triggered by a primary CIRCUIT opening, and magnetic field collapses, the high voltage arcs electricity across the spark plug's electrode GAP. When operating correctly, the coil generated spark creates sufficient heat for igniting the air/fuel mixture of the CYLINDER.

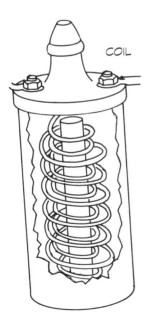

COIL

Coil Spring. A coil spring is a heat-treated, tempered SPRING that is shaped in spiral fashion. The coil spring is often used as a supporting device within a vehicle SUSPENSION system. Coil spring suspensions are sometimes used in conjunction with LEAF spring suspensions that locate at the opposite end of a vehicle. They are available in various thicknesses, lengths, and tensions. A coil spring may also be used in various parts of the vehicle to cause the mechanical RETURN action of LINKAGEs.

Suspension coil springs may lose their weight-carrying ability as they age, and the vehicle sags or lists. If a vehicle's carrying height measures inaccurately, spring strength losses should be investigated.

Cold Cranking Rate. A cold cranking rating indicates an ability of a BATTERY to crank an ENGINE when vehicle operating temperatures are cold. For example, the automobile wet-cell battery quickly loses its load-carrying capacity as temperature falls below zero degrees Fahrenheit. The rating therefore gives a sample of how much voltage and current is available at the lowered temperature. A wet-cell battery may only retain 40–50 percent of its cranking ability at extremely low temperatures. Heavy-duty batteries usually have a greater cold cranking ability than regular batteries.

Combination Valve. The combination valve is a brake pressure control VALVE that combines the actions of a PROPORTIONING VALVE and a METERING VALVE. The valve meters the amount and rate of HYDRAULIC pressures applied to the front and rear brakes of a stopping vehicle.

Combustible Mixture. A combustible mixture is composed of a mix of FUEL and air that readily burns. In automobiles the mixture is normally GASOLINE and air or DIESEL FUEL and air. In most gasoline engines, a combustible mixture ranges from rich (about 10.5 parts air to 1 part fuel) to lean (about 19.5 parts air to 1 part fuel). A mixture that ranges beyond these parameters becomes very difficult to ignite. In DIESEL ENGINEs, the fuel mixture can range from super lean (25:1) to very rich (10:1). The greater usable mixture

range of the diesel can be attributed to its very high COMPRESSION temperatures.

Combustion. Combustion is the violent joining of FUEL and OXYGEN causing heat production. In the automobile ENGINE, the rapid burning or combining of fuel and air produces heat and expands in the COMBUSTION CHAMBER. The expansion pressure pushes the engine PISTONS.

Combustion Chamber. The combustion chamber is a space in the ENGINE where COMBUSTION occurs. The chamber contains portions called quench and squish areas that carefully control the rate of fuel burning. The burn rate is carefully controlled for high efficiency and smooth pressure build-up.

Commutator. A commutator is a series of copper bars in a generator or engine starter motor ARMATURE assembly. The commutator bars are electrically insulated from the armature shaft. The bars are also insulated from one another. CARBON brushes rub against the copper bars of the commutator. The brushes form a connection between the rotating armature windings and the brush connections.

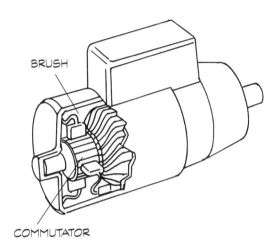

BRUSH

COMMUTATOR

CUTAWAY OF A STARTER MOTOR SHOWING
BRUSHES AND COMMUTATOR

In a generator, the MAGNETISM induces electricity that is carried from the armature through the brushes to the BATTERY. In a starter motor, the incoming electric current produces magnetism to operate the starter motor armature. The starter motor then spins the ENGINE to start its operation. *Also see* BRUSH.

Compression. A reducing of the volume space of a gaseous material by squeezing is called compression. Increasing the pressure reduces the volume and increases the density and temperature of the gaseous material. If, as in gasoline-powered engines, we compress the air and FUEL mixture to just below the IGNITION point of the fuel,

we can then add sufficient heat to start fuel burning by firing a SPARK PLUG.

In a DIESEL ENGINE, we compress only air. The air is squeezed beyond the temperature needed for fuel COMBUSTION. DIESEL FUEL is then directly injected and burning occurs automatically.

Compression Ratio. The compression ratio is the measured volume of the CYLINDER and COMBUSTION CHAMBER when an engine PISTON is at BOTTOM DEAD CENTER (BDC), divided by the volume of the combustion chamber when the piston is at TOP DEAD CENTER (TDC).

Compression Stroke. A compression stroke is the engine PISTON movement from BOTTOM DEAD CENTER (BDC) to TOP DEAD CENTER (TDC) that produces a build-up of cylinder air COMPRESSION. Since

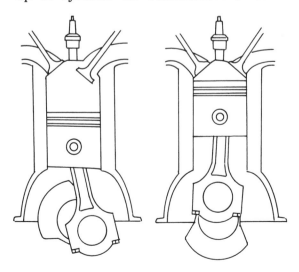

compression concentrates heat, if the compression fails to reach necessary pressures and temperatures, a CYLINDER misfire occurs.

Compressor. A compressor is a component of the AIR CONDITIONING SYSTEM that compresses REFRIGERANT vapor. The compression causes a concentration of heat. This heat is then removed to the ambient outside air via the CONDENSER, so that EVAPORATOR and vehicle interior cooling can occur.

Compressor Clutch. The compressor clutch is a magnetic coupling SOLENOID in the AIR CONDITIONING SYSTEM (A/C) that operates or disconnects the compressor DRIVESHAFT using a friction CLUTCH. When the clutch is engaged, the COMPRESSOR functions and the heated REFRIGERANT vapor is sent to the A/C CONDENSER.

Condenser. A condenser is a unit that allows a vapor to liquefy. Also, the condenser is also an electrical unit that can absorb voltage build-up.

■ In an AIR CONDITIONING SYSTEM, the condenser is a radiation-type heat exchanger that is usually located in

front of the engine RADIATOR. In the condenser, the heated and compressed REFRIGERANT vapor is cooled by air flow to return to a liquid state. The cooled liquid may then vaporize in the EVAPORATOR to absorb heat from the air flowing to the vehicle interior.

■ In older point-type IGNITION SYSTEMS, the condenser is an electrical capacitor that connects to the CONTACT POINTS. The condenser provides a storage place for the high electricity charge that occurs as the contact points open. The condenser action thereby reduces point sparking and burning from electrical ARCING.

Conductor. A conductor is a material that has a molecular construction that allows electrical current or heat to easily flow. Good electrical conductors include metals having free ELECTRONS available in their structure, such as copper, iron, and steel.

Connecting Rod. The connecting rod is an iron, steel, aluminum, or titanium rod in an ENGINE that connects a cylinder's PISTON with a JOURNAL on the engine CRANKSHAFT. The rod contains a PISTON PIN on one end and a rod BEARING on the crankshaft end. Rod bearings may be damaged by inadequate lubrication, dirty OIL, or excess heat. Rods may bend or break due to high ENGINE speed or excessive load.

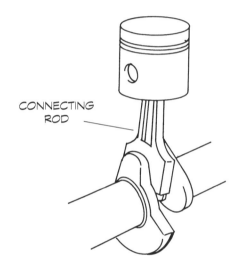

CONNECTING ROD

Constant Velocity Universal Joint. A constant velocity universal joint is a DRIVESHAFT joint manufactured so that shaft rotational pulses are lessened when the shaft transmits TORQUE through an angle. Used as DRIVELINE joints in driveshafts and AXLEs, especially in front-wheel drive vehicles, various types include the Cardan, Rzeppa, and Tripod. When worn or defective, the joints can cause driveline clicking, clanking, and vibration. If breakage occurs, serious damage may result

from driveshaft whip. Often packed with lubricant, the joint usually fails quickly when lubricant is lost through rubber boot leakage.

Any joint having a torn boot, contamination, or a dry lubricant condition should be immediately replaced.

Contact Points. Used in the BREAKER POINT IGNITION system, the points are the two stationary and movable contacts that make and break the low-voltage (primary) coil CIRCUIT. The amount of time the points connect the circuit we call the COIL build-up time. When the points open, the magnetic field of the coil collapses. The coil then fires a high secondary voltage to the SPARK PLUGs through the distributor ROTOR.

Continuous Multiport Fuel Injection (CFI, CMFI, CIS, or CIS-E). A CFI or CMFI system contains GASOLINE fuel injectors that flow FUEL continuously as the ENGINE operates. The volume of fuel that flows from the injection nozzles depends on the pressure and flow control of the fuel through lines to the injection nozzles. The fuel comes to the injection nozzles from a FUEL DISTRIBU-TOR, which despite the nomenclature, has no revolving parts. The CIS-E version added electronic OXYGEN SENSOR correction of air/fuel mixture for EMISSION CONTROLS.

Control Arm. Also called a SUSPENSION ARM, the control arm component of the vehicle SUSPENSION is designed to precisely control WHEEL movement as the vehicle moves up and down on the road. The control arm is usually supported by a shaft and BUSHING at the inboard end, and contains the BALLJOINT at the outboard end. If bushings or balljoints wear excessively, WHEEL ALIGNMENT errors result, especially in the CAMBER setting.

Controller. A controller is a computer such as an ELECTRONIC CONTROL MODULE (ECM), or ELECTRONIC CONTROL UNIT (ECU), POWERTRAIN CONTROL MODULE (PCM), or BODY CONTROL MODULE (BCM). A controller is often simply termed generically as a computer.

Control System. This term usually indicates an electrical system where output is forced to react to input. A com-puter control system has SENSORS or SWITCHes that measure various conditions, and the controller or computer calculates the needed actuator reply. Output actuators take the appropriate action.

Converter Clutch Control. *See* TORQUE CONVERTER CLUTCH.

Coolant. Coolant is a liquid mixture of ANTIFREEZE, corrosion inhibitors, anti-foaming agents, and water, which is added to water and used to carry heat out of an ENGINE.

The formula used in coolant manufacturing varies, so follow a car manufacturer or competent service technician's recommendations to add or replace coolant.

Cooling System. The cooling system removes unwanted engine heat by the circulation of air or COOLANT. In a liquid-cooled engine, the system includes coolant, a WATER PUMP, coolant passages, RADIATOR, and THERMOSTAT. In an air-cooled engine, the system usually contains a cooling FAN and air-routing ducts.

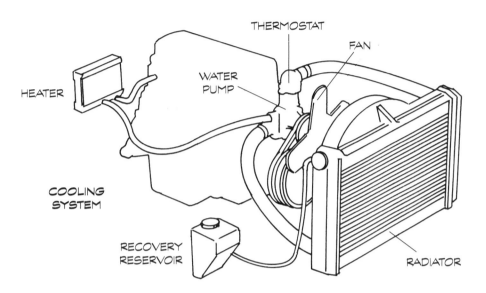

THERMOSTAT

FAN

HEATER

WATER PUMP

COOLING SYSTEM

RECOVERY RESERVOIR

RADIATOR

The cooling system's purpose is to maintain the ENGINE at an efficient operating temperature. If the engine runs too cold, poor FUEL vaporization takes place. Also, cooler temperatures allow oil contaminates to build. Engine operation should be sufficient in time to allow the engine to heat and evaporate contaminates from the engine OIL. Operating temperatures that are too hot provide poor engine fuel efficiency, oil breakdown and oil additive depletion. The thermostat is designed to maintain the optimum performance engine temperature.

The cooling system should be serviced in accordance with manufacturers recommendations.

Counter Shaft. A counter shaft is a MANUAL TRANSMISSION shaft driven by the CLUTCH SHAFT and its input gear. The counter shaft rotates in a direction counter to engine rotation. This shaft usually contains gears that supply the TRANSMISSION output shaft and vehicle DRIVETRAIN with speed reduction and TORQUE MULTIPLICATION.

Crankcase. An engine chamber that contains the CRANKSHAFT and its BEARINGS is called the crankcase. The crankcase is usually capped with the OIL PAN that covers the bottom of the ENGINE.

Crankcase Emissions. Atmospheric pollution that comes from any portion of the engine crankcase ventilating or lubricating system is called crankcase emissions. The pollution source usually comes from CYLINDER combustion gases that blow past the PISTON RINGS and add to vapors emitted from hot engine OIL.

Crankcase Ventilation. Air circulation through the CRANKCASE of a running ENGINE is called crankcase ventilation. The ventilation removes vapors and BLOWBY. The vented harmful gases are normally routed through the POSITIVE CRANKCASE VENTILATION (PCV) valve into the COMBUSTION CHAMBERS via the air intake system. In the COMBUSTION, the vapors are consumed in the burning process.

Crankshaft. The crankshaft is a steel or iron unit that serves as the main rotating shaft of the ENGINE. The crankshaft contains offset journals. Each JOURNAL is a running surface for a connecting rod BEARING. The PISTON turns the crankshaft on its main bearings. The shaft, therefore, converts piston reciprocating motion to rotary TORQUE. The torque turns the driving wheels of the vehicle through TRANSMISSION and DIFFERENTIAL gearing.

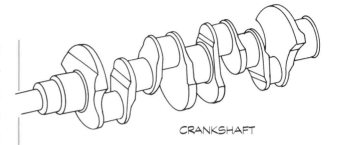

CRANKSHAFT

Crankshaft Sensor. A crankshaft sensor is a SENSOR or SWITCH that provides the engine control computer with an electrical signal. The unit pulses according to CRANKSHAFT speed and PISTON position. This unit is also called the CRANKSHAFT POSITION SENSOR (CPS).

Cruise Control. The cruise control, often termed also as a speed control, is a unit that automatically controls a vehicle's highway speed according to driver command. Early cruise control units operated via the transmission SPEEDOMETER drive cable speed, to govern the opening of the engine's THROTTLE PLATE. The cruise control would automatically open or close the throttle setting according to changes in the speedometer cable speed. Safety shut-off devices would discontinue cruise control operation if the transmission was removed from DRIVE, the BRAKES were applied, or vehicle speed dropped too low.

In late model vehicles, cruise control has become part of the computer control system. The computer, sensing ENGINE, TRANSMISSION and vehicle operations, controls the vehicle speed as set by the vehicle operator.

Curb Idle. A normal idle speed of a warmed-up, unloaded ENGINE is called the curb idle.

CV Joint. *See* CONSTANT VELOCITY UNIVERSAL JOINT.

Cycle. Events that follow in a given order are often called a cycle. In the ENGINE, four PISTON strokes work together with the ENGINE VALVES to produce four cycles of CYLINDER operation. The four cycles of engine operation are termed as the intake, COMPRESSION, power, and exhaust.

Cycling Clutch Orifice Tube (CCOT). The CCOT is an air conditioning liquid metering tube that controls the liquid REFRIGERANT flowing from the CONDENSER and vaporizing as it enters into the EVAPORATOR. The CCOT tube controls the flow as the COMPRESSOR CLUTCH automatically cycles on and off to maintain pressures and prevent either evaporator warming or icing.

Cylinder. A cylinder is a cylindrical space in the ENGINE that contains the PISTON and its PISTON RINGS. The cylinder is initially machined to a micro-finish that quickly seats the mating rings to its surface. Impregnated with engine OIL, the cylinder resists wear. To be cooled, an engine cylinder is surrounded with COOLANT passages. The cylinder can be integral, dry sleeve, or wet sleeve design.

A cylinder worn from high mileage use or loss of adequate lubrication can cause COMPRESSION loss and OIL burning.

Cylinder Block. The cylinder block is the frame of the ENGINE that contains the CRANKSHAFT, PISTONS, and CONNECTING RODS.

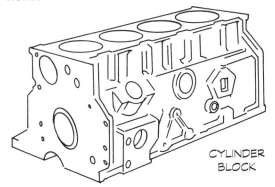

CYLINDER BLOCK

Cylinder Head. The cylinder head is the cap that covers the ENGINE BLOCK cylinders and pistons. The head can contain the coolant passages, COMBUSTION CHAMBERs, intake valves, EXHAUST VALVEs, and VALVE SEATs. If the ENGINE is air cooled, the cylinder head will contain external cooling fins.

Cylinder Identification Sensor (CID). The CID is a SENSOR that detects the engine CAMSHAFT rotational position. By doing this, the engine CYLINDER positions are detected for computer calculations of IGNITION and/or injection nozzle firings.

Cylinder Liner. *See* CYLINDER SLEEVE.

Cylinder Sleeve. A cylinder sleeve is a replaceable CYLINDER set into the CYLINDER BLOCK or frame. The sleeve forms the bore in which the PISTON reciprocates. Some cylinder sleeves are called dry sleeves, others are termed as wet sleeves. Dry sleeves are temperature fit into the block. The sleeve is chilled and slid into a highly heated block. When both sleeve and block return to normal temperatures, the sleeve is retained by frictional tightness to the block structure. If cost allows, this procedure is used by automotive machine shops to repair a severely damaged cylinder.

Wet sleeves are cylinders that nest into the block having their outer surface contacting the COOLANT. Wet sleeves are sealed against coolant leakage through the use of sealing rings located at the top and bottom sleeve circumferences.

Also, a compression sealing ring prevents COMPRESSION leaks at the cylinder sleeve. Often used in high mileage applications, such as heavy-duty DIESEL ENGINEs, the replaceable sleeves enable high-mileage use of the ENGINE BLOCK or frame.

Dashpot. A dashpot is a plunger-and-spring or DIAPHRAGM unit that controls the rate at which the THROTTLE VALVE closes. If the throttle closes too quickly, the ENGINE has a tendency to stall. The dashpot is found predominately on an engine having a CARBURETOR.

Defogger. A selected function of the air conditioner and HEATER, the defogger uses airflow to rid the windshield of fog. Air is directed by vacuum or electric SERVO doors to vent at the inside windshield surface. The air is forced through defogger/defroster ducts and out of the vents by a BLOWER MOTOR fan. *Also see* DEFROSTER.

Defroster. The defroster function of the HEATER uses engine COOLANT heat to melt frost or ice on the windshield. The heated air is blown through the HEATER CORE, which contains heated engine coolant. The air reaches the windshield through the defogger/defroster ductwork. *Also see* DEFOGGER.

Detonation. Detonation is an uncontrolled and rapid secondary explosion in the COMBUSTION CHAMBER of a SPARK IGNITION ENGINE. Detonation occurs after the SPARK PLUG fires. Also called KNOCK or PING, the noise is often confused with PRE-IGNITION sounds. Detonation can damage an engine PISTON and CONNECTING ROD. Damage may occur as sudden and rapid pressure spikes in the combustion chamber. Common causes are low-octane fuel, engine overheating and hot CARBON particles.

Diagnostic Trouble Code (DTC). *See* TROUBLE CODE.

Diagonal Brake System. A diagonal braking system is a dual circuit HYDRAULIC brake system having separate CIRCUITs that connect diagonal vehicle WHEELs together in their application (right front [RF] to left rear [LR] and left front [LF] to right rear [RR]). The diagonal feature is designed so that braking may still be supplied at the front and rear wheels after a partial hydraulic system failure.

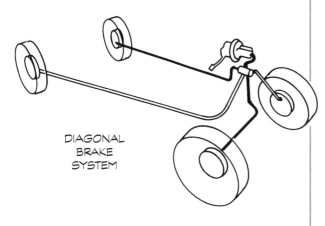

DIAGONAL
BRAKE
SYSTEM

Failure in one of the diagonal circuits is often signaled by a warning light and a lower than normal BRAKE PEDAL apply position.

Diaphragm. A diaphragm is a thin partition material that separates an area into several compartments. Used in vacuum pumps, transmission control VALVEs, SERVOs and other devices to make a mechanical response to pressure changes (air or liquid), or pump the air or liquid using mechanical means. A rupture in the thin and flexible diaphragm means a failure of unit function.

Diesel Cycle. A diesel cycle is an engine operating cycle invented by Dr. Rudolf Diesel. In the diesel cycle, intake air is tightly compressed. FUEL is then injected directly into the hot, compressed air. Spontaneous COMBUSTION occurs. The fuel, usually called DIESEL FUEL, then burns. Heat creates pressure, which pushes the engine PISTONs.

Diesel Engine. A diesel engine operates on the DIESEL CYCLE. Diesel engines burn DIESEL FUEL instead of GASOLINE. Diesel engines must withstand greater COMBUSTION pressures and TORQUE outputs than gasoline-operated counterparts. Therefore, diesels have stronger, heavier internal parts, but less revolution-per-minute tolerance.

Diesel Fuel. Diesel fuel is a light, combustible oil sprayed into the CYLINDERs of a DIESEL ENGINE near the end of the COMPRESSION STROKE. Diesel fuel is rated according to the CETANE scale.

Dieseling. Dieseling is a condition in which a SPARK IGNITION ENGINE continues to run after the ignition system SPARK PLUGs cease to fire. Dieseling is caused by cylinder CARBON deposits glowing, or hot spots in the COMBUSTION CHAMBER. These provide sufficient heat for COMBUSTION to occur. In some early pollution control vehicles, which may run hot by design, dieseling is prevented upon engine shut-down by having the THROTTLE completely close. This action cuts off all air and fuel flow.

Differential. The differential is a GEAR assembly that permits one drive AXLE to turn at a different speed than its mate while transmitting power to the wheels.

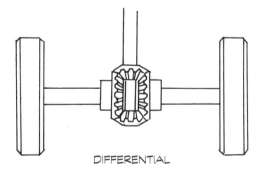

DIFFERENTIAL

Digital. A digital voltage signal is one that sequences ON and OFF, or HIGH and LOW. Digital calculations are used in computer languages.

Digital Meter. A digital meter is a meter that provides a numerical display.

Dimmer Switch. A dimmer switch is operated by the driver to manually select the high or low HEADLIGHT beam. Mounted on the driver side floorboard of older vehicles, the dimmer switch in most modern vehicles is operated by lifting the TURN SIGNAL switch lever on the STEERING COLUMN toward the driver. The late model dimmer switch is usually associated with, or part of, the turn signal switch assembly.

Diode. A diode is an electronic solid-state unit that allows electrical flow in one direction only. In automobiles, the diode is used in ALTERNATORS to change ALTERNATING CURRENT (AC) to DIRECT CURRENT (DC). The change in voltage characteristic is necessary for ELECTRIC SYSTEM operation and charging of the vehicle's BATTERY.

Direct Current (DC). An ELECTRIC CURRENT that flows ELECTRONs through a CIRCUIT in only one direction.

Direct Drive. Direct drive is a mating GEAR condition that occurs when the input speed matches the output speed. The ratio is expressed as 1:1. No TORQUE or speed value changes occur between the input and output.

Discard Thickness. Discard thickness is a minimum thickness specification for a BRAKE DISC rotor. Machining beyond this specification will cause the ROTOR to fail in use.

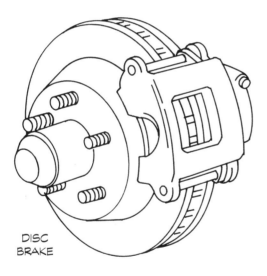

DISC
BRAKE

Disc Brake. A disc brake operates as BRAKE LINING clamps upon a plate-like disc to stop the spinning motion of the WHEEL. The disc brake is generally favored because of its high heat and water dissipation characteristics. *Also see* BRAKE DISC.

Discharge. To discharge an item is to remove the pneumatic, electrical, or HYDRAULIC PRESSURE within the system.

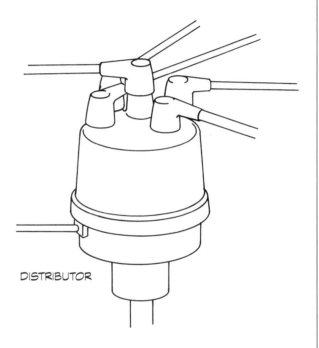

DISTRIBUTOR

Distributor. The unit that delivers ignition spark or FUEL in the automobile ENGINE.

■ In an IGNITION SYSTEM, the distributor is a rotary device that directs the high coil voltage to DISTRIBUTOR CAP terminals and the engine's SPARK PLUGS.

■ In a fuel system, a distributor delivers fuel charges to the CYLINDERs of a DIESEL ENGINE or to the intake ports of a gasoline engine.

Also see IGNITION DISTRIBUTOR *and* FUEL DISTRIBUTOR.

Distributor Cap. The distributor cap mounts on top of the IGNITION DISTRIBUTOR. The cap, usually made of an electrically resistant plastic material, houses the terminals and sockets for the ignition system's high tension (voltage) SPARK PLUG wires. Fastened to the DISTRIBUTOR body via clips or screws, the distributor cap should be inspected inside and out for terminal wear or signs of ARCING.

Arcing can cause cylinder spark plug misfire or crossfire. A distributor cap should always be kept free from moisture or dirt. Moist dirt can provide a pathway for errant high voltage flow. Also spark plug wire terminals should be clean and wire caps and boots should be in good condition.

Distributorless Ignition System (DIS). A distributorless ignition system is a spark distribution system without a mechanical IGNITION DISTRIBUTOR unit. In this system, a SENSOR sequentially signals the position of the CRANKSHAFT to a computer. The computer responds to sensor triggering by activating a primary coil winding. Each COIL fires one or two SPARK PLUGs simultaneously. DIS components are susceptible to damage, if high resistance is encountered on the secondary side. Often, the spark will jump to the module causing it to burn out.

Secondary components should be replaced on a regular basis. See manufacturer's recommendations.

Diverter Valve. In an AIR INJECTION SYSTEM, the diverter valve vents air pump output during deceleration. This venting prevents a BACKFIRE in the EXHAUST SYSTEM. This VALVE is no longer used on modern vehicles that shut off FUEL INJECTIONs during deceleration.

Drive Belt. A drive belt is a serpentine flat or V-belt that drives an accessory from the engine CRANKSHAFT pulley. The belts operate various items such as a POWER STEERING pump, air conditioning COMPRESSOR CLUTCH, and WATER PUMP.

The drive belts require periodic inspections and tension checks that may indicate an adjustment or replacement is necessary. See your vehicle manufacturer's dealer or service technician for inspection and service intervals.

Drive Chain. A drive chain transmits mechanical power. The term is sometimes used to describe the chain that operates an engine's CAMSHAFT. *See* TIMING CHAIN.

Driveline. The DRIVESHAFT, UNIVERSAL JOINT, SLIP JOINT, and AXLE units that form the flow path for driving TORQUE to the vehicle wheels.

Driven Disc. *See* FRICTION DISC.

Drive Pinion. A rotating GEAR that transmits TORQUE to another gear. The driven gear is usually called the RING GEAR. Used in final drive gears in the drive AXLE, sometimes called the THIRD MEMBER, the drive pinion is supported by two BEARINGS.

Driveshaft. The driveshaft is a metal or fiber tube having one or two UNIVERSAL JOINTs. The driveshaft transmits power from a TRANSMISSION to the drive axle PINION GEAR. *Also see* PROPELLER SHAFT.

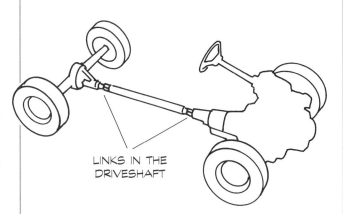

LINKS IN THE
DRIVESHAFT

Drivetrain. The vehicle drivetrain transmits engine TORQUE to the road. The components of the drivetrain consist of the ENGINE, the CLUTCH or TORQUE CONVERTER, the TRANSMISSION, DRIVESHAFT(s), DIFFERENTIAL, drive AXLEs, and DRIVE WHEELS.

Drive Wheels. Wheels that apply the driving force of the ENGINE to the ground surface are called the drive wheels.

Drum Brake. A drum brake assembly consists of the convex, curved metal brake SHOEs and brake friction linings that press against the inner circumference of a metal BRAKE DRUM when

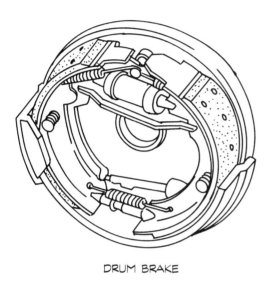

DRUM BRAKE

applied. The BRAKE LINING application's frictional contact produces the drum brake and wheel stopping action.

DTC. Diagnostic Trouble Code. *See* TROUBLE CODES.

Dwell. Dwell is the amount of time that the primary current of the IGNITION SYSTEM passes through a closed SWITCH (such as the ELECTRONIC CONTROL MODULE).

Dynamic Balance. The balance of a rotating mass when it is in motion is called dynamic balance, such as the dynamic balance of a CRANKSHAFT or a rotating vehicle WHEEL. Dynamic balance is usually critical to prevent vibrations in high-speed components.

Eccentric. An eccentric is an offset shape used to convert rotary motion to reciprocating motion. *See* CAM *and* CAMSHAFT.

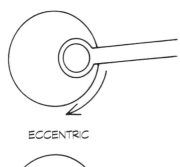

ECCENTRIC

ECM. Also called the Electronic Control Unit (ECU) or Powertrain Control Module (PCM). *Also see* ELECTRONIC CONTROL MODULE *and* POWERTRAIN CONTROL MODULE.

ECU. Abbreviation for Electronic Control Unit. *See* ELECTRONIC CONTROL MODULE.

EGR. *See* EXHAUST GAS RECIRCULATION.

Electric Current. Measured in AMPERES, electric current is the flow of ELECTRONS through a CONDUCTOR such as a copper wire. In application, electrical power transmits using alternating current (AC) or direct current (DC). *See* ALTERNATING CURRENT *and* DIRECT CURRENT.

Electric System. The electric system provides automobile electricity for cranking and starting the ENGINE, firing SPARK PLUGS, charging the BATTERY, and operating lights and other electrical equipment.

Electrode. An electrode is an electric terminal built to produce and carry an electric arc across an air GAP. For example, a spark jumps between two ELECTRODES in a SPARK PLUG. The heat produced fires the FUEL in the CYLINDER.

Electrolyte. Electrolyte is the liquid mixture in a vehicle BATTERY. Elec-

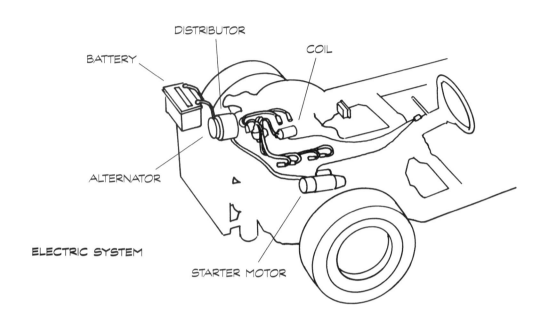

ELECTRIC SYSTEM

(Labels: BATTERY, DISTRIBUTOR, COIL, ALTERNATOR, STARTER MOTOR)

trolyte consists of approximately 60 percent water and 40 percent SULFURIC ACID in a fully-charged vehicle battery. The acid enters into chemical reaction with active material in the lead PLATEs to store electric voltage potential.

Battery acids are to be handled with extreme caution. Chemical burns may result from contact. Especially guard physically sensitive areas, such as eyes, if you work around the wet cell battery. If acid exposure contacts eyes or sensitive areas, immediate medical attention is recommended. Do not touch the acid or acid residue build-up on battery terminals. Also, clothing may be damaged by BATTERY ACID.

Electromagnet. A COIL of wire, usually wrapped around an iron core, that produces MAGNETISM as electric current passes through the wire.

Electromagnetic Induction. Electromagnetic induction is the magnetic field characteristic that causes ELECTRIC CURRENT in a CONDUCTOR as the conductor passes through the magnetic field. INDUCTION is also produced if the magnetic field builds and collapses around the conductor.

Electron. An electron is a negatively charged atomic particle. The electron circles the nucleus of an atom. If loosened in orbit by external force, electron current flow can result. We measure electric current using the AMPERE measurement scale.

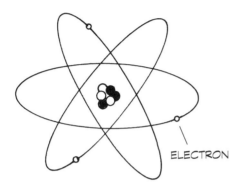

ELECTRON

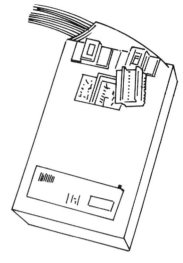

ELECTRONIC CONTROL MODULE

Electronic. That which pertains to electrons and electricity is often called electronic. Today the term primarily indicates solid-state or microcircuit components.

Electronic Control Module (ECM). The electronic control module is the computer that receives information from various SENSORs and operates on-board vehicle systems, CIRCUITs, and actuators. Once used singularly and primarily for electronic IGNITION or FUEL INJECTION control, late model vehicles may have several variously named control modules or computers for different systems. Also called ELECTRONIC CONTROL UNIT.

Electronic Control Unit (ECU). *See* ELECTRONIC CONTROL MODULE (ECM).

Electronic Engine Control (EEC). An electronic engine control system uses various SENSORs and SWITCHes to send or input electrical signals to the ELECTRONIC CONTROL MODULE or POWERTRAIN CONTROL MODULE. The computer then calculates output signals that are sent to various actuators such as those that control the IGNITION COIL(s), FUEL INJECTION, and EMISSION CONTROL systems.

Electronic Fuel Injection (EFI). An electronic fuel injection system injects FUEL into the ENGINE using an electronic computer to time and meter the fuel flow. In recent years, EFI is incorporated in with the POWERTRAIN CONTROL MODULE function.

Electronic Ignition. An electronic ignition system uses DIODES, TRANSISTORS, or other semiconductor devices as electronic SWITCHES. The switches turn the primary COIL current on and off in time with ENGINE rotation.

Electronic Ride Control. Electronic ride control is a system that automatically changes the firmness of vehicle SHOCK ABSORBERS to suit various vehicle ride conditions.

Electronic Spark Timing (EST). Electronic spark timing monitors engine load, speed, and temperature, to send electric signals to an ELECTRONIC CONTROL UNIT (ECU, ECM, or PCM). The computer electronically provides proper ignition SPARK ADVANCE for good exhaust quality, fuel economy, and performance characteristics.

Emission Control. An emission control is a device on a motor vehicle designed for the reduction of air polluting emissions from the ENGINE or FUEL TANK.

Endplay. Endplay is the CLEARANCE dis-

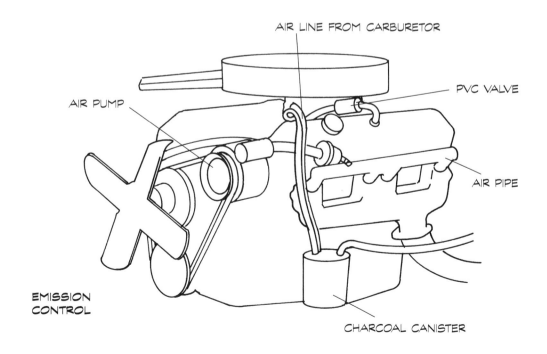

AIR LINE FROM CARBURETOR

PVC VALVE

AIR PUMP

AIR PIPE

EMISSION
CONTROL

CHARCOAL CANISTER

tance between parts that allows a shaft to move forward or backward in its housing.

Energy. The potential ability to accomplish work is called energy. Common energy forms are mechanical, light, heat, electrical, and chemical.

Engine. The engine is a machine categorized as a prime mover, having the ability to convert a FUEL's heat energy to mechanical energy. In the automobile, the engine produces the power to move the vehicle. Also called the MOTOR.

Engine Block. The engine block is the central portion of the ENGINE that contains the CYLINDERS, PISTONS, CONNECTING RODS, and CRANKSHAFT. Depending on design, the engine block may locate the cylinders in an in-line, V-style, or opposed-cylinder configuration. The block may be liquid or air cooled, and usually contains internal circuits for the distribution of the engine lubricating OIL.

Engine Coolant-Temperature Sensor (ECT or CTS). The ECT is a thermally

sensitive electric resistor (THERMISTOR) located in the COOLING SYSTEM that reports engine COOLANT temperature to the engine control computer and INSTRUMENT PANEL.

Engine Cradle. The engine cradle is a sub-frame that fastens under the front of the vehicle body. Using rubber mounts, the cradle may hold the ENGINE or the engine/TRANSAXLE assembly in place.

Engine Mounts. Engine mounts are rubber or hydraulic vibration or movement absorbers. Engine mounts are units through which the ENGINE is bolted into the vehicle FRAME, sub-frame, cradle, or body. They absorb the TORQUE reactions of the engine.

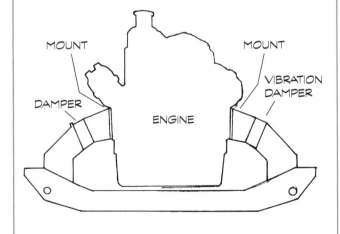

ENGINE MOUNTS

Engine Valve. The engine valve controls the flow of air or air/fuel mixture to the engine's CYLINDER, and spent exhaust gases from the cylinder. The engine valve is made high alloy steel for wear resistance. The INTAKE VALVE admits an air/fuel mixture into the cylinder, or just air if the engine is a DIESEL ENGINE. The exhaust valve allows the exit of spent combustion gases through the EXHAUST SYSTEM.

Engine valve life may be shortened by inadequate valve cooling. This may be caused by improper VALVE SEAT contact or excess COMBUSTION CHAMBER temperatures. In valve burning, the outer edge of the poppet-style VALVE HEAD burns away. This allows cylinder COMPRESSION losses and misfire.

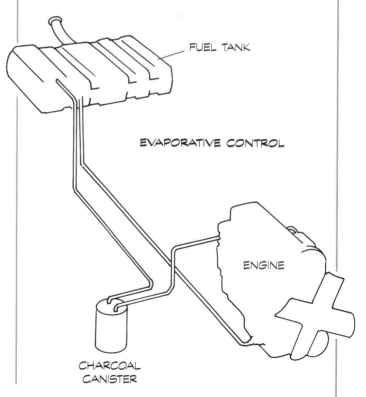

Cylinder efficiency, compression, and leakage tests can usually determine engine VALVE SEAT and SEAL problems.

Evacuating. Used to describe a VACUUM pump process, evacuating rids the AIR CONDITIONING SYSTEM of unwanted air and moisture. Evacuation is usually accomplished after air conditioning repairs are complete, before the system receives a fresh charge of REFRIGERANT.

Evaporative Control. The evaporative control system is an air pollution control that prevents the escape of fuel vapors from the FUEL TANK, engine CRANKCASE, or intake AIR CLEANER. Commonly, in an engine evaporative control, fuel vapors store in a CHARCOAL CANISTER while the engine is off, and are purged through the COMBUSTION CHAMBERS when the engine runs.

FUEL TANK

EVAPORATIVE CONTROL

ENGINE

CHARCOAL
CANISTER

Evaporator. The evaporator is a heat exchanger found in the air conditioning refrigerant CIRCUIT that allows the liquid REFRIGERANT to change to a GAS. The evaporation removes heat from the air that enters the vehicle passenger compartment.

Exhaust Analyzer. An exhaust analyzer is a tester that measures the amounts of air pollutants in vehicle exhaust gases. Analyzers commonly used in automotive shops measure HYDROCARBONS (HC), CARBON MONOXIDE (CO), OXYGEN (O₂), CARBON DIOXIDE (CO₂), and NITROGEN OXIDES (NOx).

Exhaust Cycle. An exhaust cycle is the duration of time that the spent exhaust gases from a CYLINDER can escape through an open EXHAUST VALVE. The exhaust cycle is usually slightly longer in CRANKSHAFT rotation than the piston's EXHAUST STROKE.

Exhaust Emissions. Exhaust emissions are unwanted COMBUSTION by-products. Common pollutants are NITROGEN OXIDES (NOx), unburned HYDROCARBONS (HC), and CARBON MONOXIDE (CO).

Exhaust Gas Recirculation (EGR).

Exhaust gas recirculation (EGR) is a pollution control system that reduces NITROGEN OXIDES (NOx) exhaust emissions. The EGR recycles a portion of the hot, spent, and inert exhaust gases back through the engine CYLINDER. This action displaces excess OXYGEN and quenches very high cylinder temperatures that can cause NOx to form.

Exhaust Gas Recirculation Valve Position Sensor (EVP). The EVP reports the position of the EGR valve to the ELECTRONIC CONTROL MODULE (ECM) or POWERTRAIN CONTROL MODULE (PCM).

Exhaust Manifold. The exhaust manifold is a hollow piping device, made of steel tubing or cast iron, having passages through which engine exhaust gases can escape the COMBUSTION CHAMBERS. Often sealed in by manifold GASKETs, high COMBUSTION heat passes through the exhaust manifold to the MUFFLER and CATALYTIC CONVERTER.

The exhaust manifold should not operate near units affected by heat. Therefore, the exhaust manifold or manifold pipes may be surrounded by heat deflectors. The deflectors protect nearby components.

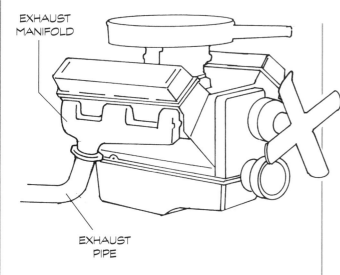

EXHAUST
MANIFOLD

EXHAUST
PIPE

To prevent burns, the exhaust manifold should not be touched during engine operation or shortly thereafter, until cooling occurs.

Exhaust Pipe. The exhaust pipe connects the engine's EXHAUST MANIFOLD to the next part in the EXHAUST SYSTEM, usually a CATALYTIC CONVERTER or MUFFLER.

Exhaust Stroke. The exhaust stroke occurs as the PISTON strokes from BOTTOM DEAD CENTER (BDC) connecting rod bearing position, to the TOP DEAD CENTER (TDC) bearing position with the EXHAUST VALVE lifted off its seat. The exhaust stroke immediately follows the down-ward POWER STROKE and precedes the INTAKE STROKE. A stroke is always 180 degrees of CRANKSHAFT rotation.

Exhaust System. The exhaust system collects engine CYLINDER exhaust gases and discharges them into the air. The exhaust system begins at the EXHAUST MANIFOLD. The manifold routes the spent exhaust gases to the EXHAUST PIPE, the CATALYTIC CONVERTER, MUFFLER, TAILPIPE, and possibly a RESONATOR. The exhaust system should be inspected on a regular basis. Any damaged items should be replaced.

Exhaust Valve. The exhaust valve is a poppet type VALVE, usually located in the CYLINDER HEAD, that controls the exit of spent exhaust gases from the CYLINDER. The exhaust valve is opened by a CAM LOBE and its attending VALVETRAIN components. The exhaust valve is closed by the exhaust valve SPRING. Subject to burning because of improper contact with the VALVE SEAT area, the exhaust valve may leak COMPRESSION and COMBUSTION pressures into the EXHAUST MANIFOLD. As well, subject to excess VALVE GUIDE wear at its stem, the valve can wobble, improperly seat, and burn.

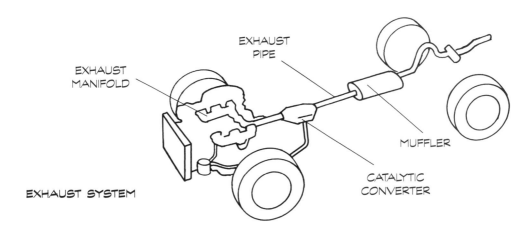

EXHAUST
PIPE

EXHAUST
MANIFOLD

MUFFLER

CATALYTIC
CONVERTER

EXHAUST SYSTEM

Expansion Plug. Sometimes called a freeze plug, an expansion plug seals holes in the ENGINE BLOCK and CYLINDER HEAD formed during metal casting. The plug often provides a force relief if a COOLING SYSTEM freezes. The expansion plug pops out of the hole in the block or head and cast metal breakage is often prevented.

The expansion plugs may corrode on high-mileage vehicles and require replacement if COOLANT leaks occur.

Expansion Tank. An expansion tank is a COOLING SYSTEM reservoir that connects by hose to the filler neck of the engine's RADIATOR. The reservoir provides room for the expansion of heated COOLANT. The radiator cap allows flow to the tank when the coolant system pressurizes to the level of the cap spring. The cap also allows the return of this coolant to the system as engine cooling takes place.

Expansion Valve. An expansion valve is a refrigerant flow control VALVE located between the air conditioning system's CONDENSER and EVAPORATOR. The expansion valve, also termed as the THERMOSTATIC EXPANSION VALVE (TXV), controls the amount of REFRIGERANT sprayed into the evaporator for vehicle passenger cooling.

A failed valve can cause poor interior cooling or freezing of the air humidity in the evaporator. Freezing can impede air flowing into the vehicle interior.

Fan. A fan is an IMPELLER blade-equipped air pumping device. Fans commonly used in the automobile include:

■ The radial fan in front of, or behind, the engine-cooling RADIATOR. The fan pushes or pulls air through the radiator. The fan may be directly driven by the engine CRANKSHAFT using a belt, or through a belt-driven CLUTCH mecha-

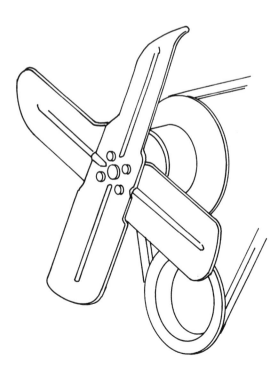

nism. A cooling fan may also be powered by an electric MOTOR on newer vehicles, especially if the vehicle is transverse engine-equipped.

■ The air blower centrifugal fan that drives air into the vehicle passenger compartment. The BLOWER fan is an electric motor-driven unit. The fan has a squirrel cage blade design and is mounted within the heater/air conditioning housing.

Fan Belt. The fan belt is a belt that drives the engine cooling FAN of most longitudinally positioned engines. Belts may also drive the WATER PUMP, ALTERNATOR, air conditioning COMPRESSOR, POWER STEERING pump, air injection pump, and/or VACUUM pump. The belt may be V-belt or serpentine belt design.

Fan belts need periodic adjustment or replacement according to vehicle mileage and age. Check the vehicle manufacturer recommendations to check the intervals required.

Feedback Carburetor. A feedback carburetor is an air/fuel mixing device containing mixture adjustment abilities. The CARBURETOR, having a MIXTURE CONTROL SOLENOID or METERING VALVE to adjust air/fuel mixture, is used with electronic fuel control systems to adjust the AIR/FUEL RATIO for maximum CATALYTIC CONVERTER efficiency.

Field Coil. A field coil is a GENERATOR or starting motor electrical COIL or winding.

Filter. A filter is a device through which air, gases, or liquids are passed to remove particle impurities.

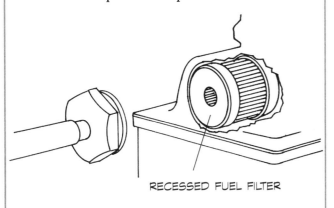

RECESSED FUEL FILTER

Automotive filters require regular replacement service intervals. Check your vehicle service manual for recommendations.

Final Drive Ratio. The final drive ratio is the speed reduction available in the DIFFERENTIAL. The ratio is expressed in a GEAR RATIO such as 3.55 to 1.

Firing Order. The firing order is the sequential order in which the engine cylinders fire, beginning with the number one CYLINDER. The interval between firings depends on the number of cylinders an ENGINE contains. In a FOUR-CYCLE engine, all cylinders fire in two rotations (720 degrees) of the engine CRANKSHAFT.

Fixed Caliper. A DISC BRAKE caliper mounted solidly in a fixed position in respect to disc ROTATION is called the fixed caliper. The CALIPER cannot move. The fixed caliper contains two or four opposing PISTONs. When the BRAKE applies, the pistons push the BRAKE LINING toward two opposing sides of the disc, squeezing the BRAKE DISC to slow or stop its spin.

Flasher. A flasher is a CIRCUIT BREAKER that automatically switches electricity on and off. The flasher supplies power to the TURN SIGNAL and HAZARD WARNING LIGHT circuits. A flasher unit may also be used to operate an anti-theft warning horn circuit.

Flex Plate. The flex plate is a thin drive plate bolted to the TRANSMISSION end of an engine CRANKSHAFT. Used with AUTOMATIC TRANSMISSIONS, the flex plate transfers engine TORQUE to the transmission's TORQUE CONVERTER or FLUID COUPLING. The flex plate attaches to the crankshaft via hardened and safety-keyed bolts. The flex plate attaches to the torque converter using bolts or nuts and mating studs at the outer circumference.

The tightening torque used for flex plate installation during repairs is extremely important, and should be applied with a torque wrench.

Float Bowl. The portion of the CARBURETOR that contains FUEL is called the float bowl. Using a float, the bowl maintains an appropriate fuel level through the use of an inlet needle and its seat. The needle and seat are usually replaced during carburetor overhaul.

Floating Caliper. A floating caliper is a movable DISC BRAKE caliper. A floating caliper has either one large single hydraulic PISTON, or two smaller hydraulic pistons. When operated by hydraulic braking pressure, the caliper piston(s) pushes a BRAKE PAD against one surface of the BRAKE DISC. The push causes the CALIPER to react and slide on the BUSHINGs and pins, slides, or RACES. The caliper floats laterally and applies the opposing brake disc to the brake ROTOR. The squeeze clamps the brake friction lining on the disc to slow or stop its motion. A floating caliper can prematurely wear BRAKE LINING if the slide pins or races fail to properly allow caliper movement.

Fluid Coupling. A fluid coupling is a unit that mechanically transmits TORQUE though the use of fluid momentum. Using the laws of hydrodynamics, the fluid coupling contains an IMPELLER and TURBINE. The fluid coupling is a round, donut-shaped housing filled with fluid. In the fluid, two FANs are positioned facing each other. In automotive use, the coupling is filled with transmission fluid.

The engine's CRANKSHAFT drives the impeller fan. Equipped with VANE blades, the impeller throws the fluid into the turbine using centrifugal force. The fluid expends its centrifugal force energy on the blades of the turbine. Torque is therefore transmitted to the turbine blades. The turbine's OUTPUT SHAFT is located at the turbine's center to carry the torque to the TRANSMISSION.

Though some early AUTOMATIC TRANS-MISSION-equipped vehicles contained a fluid coupling, the unit is far surpassed in efficiency by the torque converter. *See* TORQUE CONVERTER.

Flywheel. A flywheel is a heavy metal disc attached to the engine CRANKSHAFT output end. The flywheel rotates with the crankshaft and helps smooth CYLINDER power surges. The flywheel usually contains outer circumference starter ring teeth. The STARTER MOTOR drive gear engages the teeth to crank the ENGINE. The flywheel also sports a machined flat surface for the engagement of the CLUTCH DISC. The disc feeds engine TORQUE to the MANUAL TRANSMISSION.

Occasionally flywheel surface wear or scoring demands flywheel resurfacing or replacement. The flywheel should be replaced or resurfaced during CLUTCH replacement.

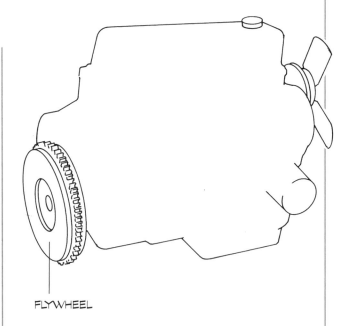

FLYWHEEL

Follower. The follower is a cylindrical device that rides on the CAM LOBE of an ENGINE, to follow the cam lobe profile. The follower, therefore, changes the rotary motion of the cam lobe to linear motion in the VALVETRAIN. The linear motion operates the valvetrain components against VALVE SPRING pressure and opens the VALVE. In an engine, the follower is also often called a LIFTER.

Four-Cycle. The four-cycle events are the four breathing actions caused by the vehicle's engine PISTON strokes. These cycles are: intake, compression, power, and exhaust. These produce the complete cycle of events for the operation of the four-cycle engine. Though not exactly synonymous terms, an ENGINE may be termed interchangeably as a four-cycle engine or FOUR-STROKE engine.

Four-Stroke. A stroke is the physical up or down action of a PISTON and CONNECTING ROD assembly within a FOUR-CYCLE engine. Lasting exactly 180 degrees of CRANKSHAFT revolution, each stroke is termed similarly to its corresponding cycle of the engine operation. The four-stroke sequence of strokes are: intake, compression, power, and exhaust.

Four-Wheel Alignment. Four-wheel alignment is a WHEEL ALIGNMENT process that checks the alignment angle of both front and rear WHEELS. This adds the process of checking and adjusting of rear wheel CASTER, TOE, and TRACKING to the alignment.

 Alignment should be checked and adjusted on a regular basis.

Four-Wheel Drive (4WD). Four-wheel drive is used to describe a vehicle having driving axles at both front and rear of the vehicle, so that either two wheels or all four wheels may provide motive power. The vehicle DRIVETRAIN usually includes a shifting mechanism to change operation between TWO-WHEEL DRIVE (2WD) and 4WD function. The shift changes power flow though the TRANSMISSION and a TRANSFER CASE. Many 4WD vehicles also have a mechanism in the front AXLE assembly to disconnect the front wheel gearing for fuel economy purposes. Some vehicles have F4WD operation, meaning that the 4WD has a full-time function.

Frame. Frame is a term used to describe the structural support in a vehicle with body-over frame construction. The frame is the strong metal structure to which the body, ENGINE, TRANSMISSION, or TRANSAXLE and other parts are attached.

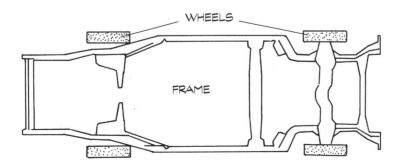

Free Travel. The distance a mechanical object can move before creating a reaction. Free travel is sometimes called LASH or PLAY.

■ In the HYDRAULIC BRAKE system, free travel is the distance the BRAKE PEDAL moves before the primary seals in the MASTER CYLINDER close hydraulic vent PORTs and apply the BRAKES.

■ In gearing, free travel is the amount the input device moves before the meshing output part begins to produce power transfer.

Friction. Friction is the RESISTANCE to motion occurring between two material bodies rubbing in contact with each other.

Friction Disc. A friction disc is used in a dry or wet (oiled) CLUTCH. The friction disc is coated or covered on both sides with friction material. The inner HUB is splined to a hub or shaft. The two flat surfaces of friction lining are squeezed to a metal plate or FLYWHEEL by a clutch or PISTON. The friction disc then correlates hub speed and the driving plate speed. The friction disc is also called a DRIVEN DISC or CLUTCH DISC. Friction disc materials are sensitive to

PLAY adjustment error, overheating, and wear.

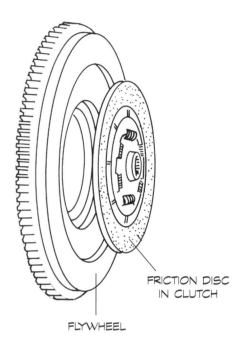

FRICTION DISC
IN CLUTCH

FLYWHEEL

Front-End Alignment. The angular relationship between the front WHEELS, the vehicle body or FRAME, and the roadway is called front-end alignment. Alignment angles include CAMBER, CASTER, TOE, STEERING AXIS INCLINATION, and TURNING RADIUS. Front-wheel alignment is now superseded by a four-wheel alignment, especially in FRONT-WHEEL DRIVE vehicles. Alignment should be checked and adjusted on a regular basis. *Also see* FOUR WHEEL ALIGNMENT.

Front-Wheel Drive (FWD). A front-wheel drive vehicle has its motive force applied to the roadway through the vehicle's front wheels. The FWD vehicle has gained wide use through its innate ability to increase fuel mileage over REAR-WHEEL DRIVE (RWD) vehicles. The fuel mileage increase is credited to the FWD's shorter and lighter DRIVELINE.

Fuel. Fuel is a combustible chemical. In a SPARK IGNITION ENGINE, it's GASOLINE. Propane, natural gas, or a similar fuel vapor burns to produce heat. Heated air expansion pushes the engine PISTONS. In a DIESEL ENGINE, COMPRESSION heat ignites the fuel as it is injected directly into the CYLINDER.

Fuel Distributor. A fuel distributor is a device used to deliver FUEL to the injection NOZZLES of an ENGINE.

■ In the gasoline engine, the fuel distributor can deliver variable pressure or timed fuel charge amounts to injection nozzles mounted in the engine intake air passages.

■ In DIESEL ENGINES, the fuel distributor delivers timed high pressure (approximately 1500-2500 psi). Fuel charges directly to the injection noz-

zles located in the engine CYLINDERS or PRE-COMBUSTION CHAMBERS.

Fuel Filter. The fuel filter is a device in the fuel delivery line that removes solid contaminates from the FUEL. Filters may be rated according to their micron filtration abilities.

 Fuel filters are recommended for replacement at mileage intervals. Check with the vehicle manufacturer or a service technician for service recommendations.

Fuel Hose. A fuel hose is a reinforced rubber hose specifically designed for carrying fuel system pressures.

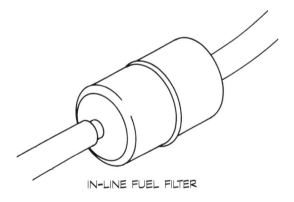

IN-LINE FUEL FILTER

Always ensure that a replacement fuel hose is rated to carry the operating fuel system pressures. Never allow replacement of a fuel hose with a vacuum hose.

Fuel Injection. A fuel injection system delivers metered FUEL under pressure through injection NOZZLEs or injectors into the engine's INTAKE MANIFOLD or COMBUSTION CHAMBER. The result of injection is a fine mist of fuel that quickly atomizes and vaporizes when exposed to heat.

Fuel Line. A fuel line is a steel tube delivering FUEL to the ENGINE from the FUEL TANK. Also, a fuel line returns unused or excess fuel back to the tank.

During vehicle repair, copper tubing should never be used as a replacement fuel line.

Fuel Pressure Regulator. A fuel pressure regulator is a spring-loaded mechanical device used to maintain or

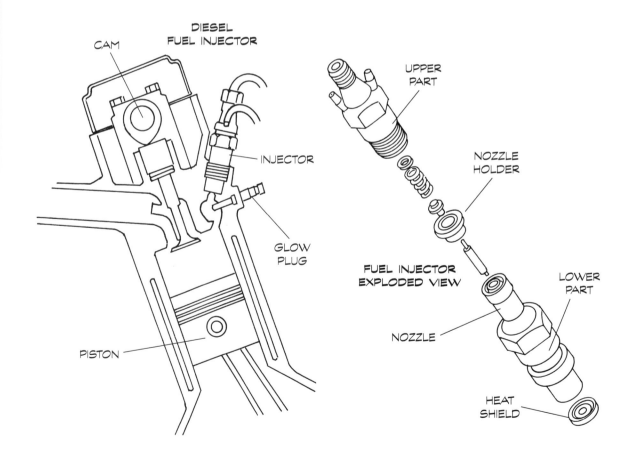

DIESEL
FUEL INJECTOR

CAM

INJECTOR

GLOW
PLUG

PISTON

UPPER
PART

NOZZLE
HOLDER

FUEL INJECTOR
EXPLODED VIEW

LOWER
PART

NOZZLE

HEAT
SHIELD

control fuel pressure. Primarily used in FUEL INJECTION systems, the regulator may contain either a flexible DIAPHRAGM or mechanical VALVE. The valve accomplishes regulation through the movement of a pressure bleed, which flows fuel back to the FUEL TANK or inlet of the FUEL PUMP. The regulator may have a static pressure relief level, or a pressure level adjusted by a VACUUM or BOOST pressure.

Fuel Pump. The fuel pump is an electrical or mechanical unit in the fuel system that forces FUEL to flow from the FUEL TANK to the CARBURETOR or FUEL INJECTION system. Carbureted engines normally possess a mechanical spring-diaphragm fuel pump driven from the engine CAMSHAFT. Fuel injection engines usually use a frame-, body-, or tank-mounted electric fuel pump.

⚠ It is recommended that FUEL LINES not be opened by untrained persons because the resulting spray is highly flammable.

Fuel Tank. The fuel tank is a reservoir for holding the engine FUEL until it is consumed in the engine COMBUSTION

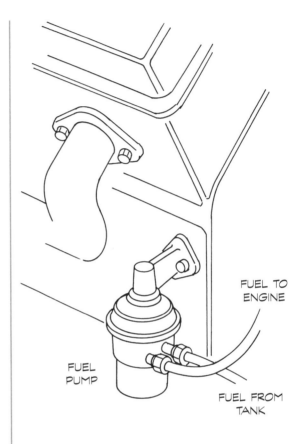

FUEL TO ENGINE

FUEL PUMP

FUEL FROM TANK

process. The tank normally has a filler tube, where the tank is filled, and normally three smaller hose connections. The first of the three smaller hoses is the fuel outlet that feeds the fuel to the FUEL PUMP. The fuel outlet or supply tube begins the flow deep in the tank's bottom. Here a sock-like filter element filters dirt out as the system pump picks up the fuel. The fuel flows through the fuel pump, and an in-line

FUEL FILTER, to the engine FUEL INJECTION system or CARBURETOR inlet.

The second tube, usually larger in diameter than the first, vents fuel vapors to the CHARCOAL CANISTER. Fuel vapors—air pollutants if they escape—are absorbed and stored by the charcoal as the vehicle sits. These vapors are purged into the engine to be consumed when it starts.

Lastly, the third line is a fuel return line. In fuel injected systems, in particular, much of the fuel that is delivered through the fuel pump returns to the fuel tank, the engine consuming only the fuel needed for its operation.

Fuse. A fuse is a device that opens an electric CIRCUIT when excessive current flows. The fuse will carry less current than the circuit's components, to protect equipment in the circuit. If excess current flows, the fuse melts or "blows."

The source of fuse failure should be found before a new fuse is installed. Replacement fuses must be of the same amp rating. A fuse may be mounted either in-line (in a wire) or in a FUSE BLOCK.

Fuse Block. A fuse block is a panel that holds many FUSEs, or CIRCUIT BREAKERs, for the various electric circuits of a vehicle.

Fusible Link. A fusible link is a short length of wire connected in series with an electrical circuit. Acting much like a FUSE, the link melts when excessive current flows and protects electrical components.

Never replace a fusible link with standard wiring, as serious electrical damage or fire may occur. *Also see* FUSE *and* FUSE BLOCK.

Gap. A gap is an air space between electrode terminals, such as the SPARK PLUG gap.

Gas. A gas is matter that has neither definite shape nor volume. In automobiles:

■ Discharge from the TAILPIPE is called exhaust gas. Exhaust gas has harmful compounds and gases within its chemistry.

■ Liquid FUEL is called GASOLINE or gas. Not extremely gaseous at room temperatures, gasoline is made from crude oil HYDROCARBONS that vaporize quickly at higher-than-room-temperatures. *See* GASOLINE.

■ Refrigerant gases are found in the AIR CONDITIONING SYSTEM. Older vehicles may contain a REFRIGERANT gas that is harmful to the environment. This older gas, called R-12, must be replaced during air conditioning system repair. The refrigerant gas may be vapor or liquid, depending on the refrigerant circuit pressure and temperature.

Gasket. A gasket is a layer of soft material, such as paper, rubber, cork, copper, synthetic materials, or a combination of these materials, that is placed between two solid parts. The gasket provides a tight joint SEAL when the parts are connected with proper pressure or tension.

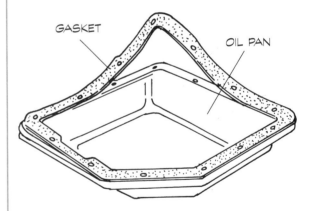

GASKET

OIL PAN

Gasoline. Gasoline is used as a FUEL in most automobile engines. It is a liquid HYDROCARBON obtained from crude oil. Gasoline is given an OCTANE RATING that compares it to isooctane, a stable hydrocarbon with very high anti-KNOCK proprieties.

Gear. A gear is a rotary wheel having teeth that MESH with the teeth of another gear. Together the gear-set transmits turning force (TORQUE) from the driving gear to the driven gear.

Gear Lubricant. A gear lubricant is a GREASE or OIL designed especially for MANUAL TRANSMISSIONS, TRANSAXLES, and rear axles. Gear lubricants, often called gear "lube" by mechanics, have important VISCOSITY (thickness) ratings, and additives to help in the material's service life.

🚙 TRANSMISSION and AXLE lubricants require replacement on a regular basis. Check with the vehicle manufacturer or a service technician for service recommendations.

Gear Ratio. The gear ratio is the revolutions a driving GEAR must turn to make a driven gear complete one revolution. The ratio is found by dividing the number of teeth on the driven gear by teeth counted on the driving gear.

Gearshift. A gearshift is a mechanism through which GEARs or ranges in an automotive TRANSMISSION are engaged and disengaged. A gearshift is usually a STEERING COLUMN or floor-mounted lever.

Generator. A generator is a unit that converts mechanical energy into electric energy using MAGNETIC FORCE. If producing ALTERNATING CURRENT, a generator is usually called an ALTERNATOR. Automotive generators produce either 6 or 12 volt DC current.

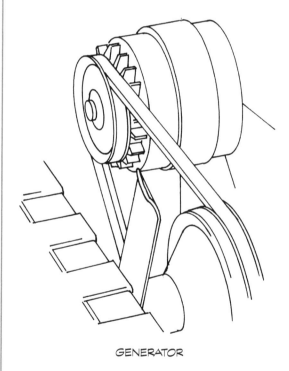

GENERATOR

Glow Plug. A glow plug is an electric HEATER that operates in the PRECOMBUSTION CHAMBERS of DIESEL ENGINEs before starting. The glow plug preheats the chamber for easier engine starting in cold weather.

Goober. In mechanic's slang, a goober is a vehicle having an elusive diagnostic problem.

Governor. A governor is a device that controls another device. For example:

■ In the DIESEL ENGINE, the governor usually controls the engine's revolutions per minute on the basis of speed or load.

■ The AUTOMATIC TRANSMISSION governor energizes shifting according to road speed.

■ A vehicle speed governor or SENSOR may sense highway speeds to provide a throttle CRUISE CONTROL or electronic control of automatic transmission shifting.

Grease. Grease is a petroleum or synthetic OIL to which thickening agents have been added. Grease provides good high-load bearing lubrication. WHEEL BEARING grease, for example, is

designed for FRICTION reduction under high-speed and high-temperature BEARING operations.

Ground. The ground is the return path to the BATTERY for current in an electric CIRCUIT. The ground circuit, often the metal vehicle FRAME or body in vehicles, is usually polarized as NEGATIVE. A ground path to the vehicle battery normally requires no protective insulation.

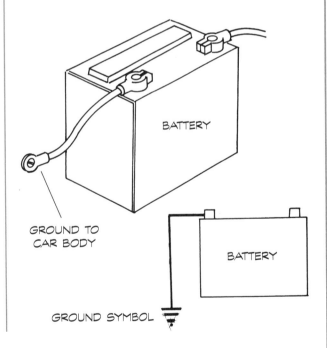

GROUND TO CAR BODY

BATTERY

BATTERY

GROUND SYMBOL

Halfshafts. Used in front drive, all-wheel, 4x4, and independent rear SUSPENSIONs, halfshafts connect from a TRANSAXLE or DIFFERENTIAL to the vehicle's driving WHEELs. Normally, halfshafts contain SPLINEs, and UNIVERSAL JOINTs or CONSTANT VELOCITY UNIVERSAL (CV) JOINTs.

Hall-Effect Switch. A Hall-Effect switch is a SWITCH that responds to magnetic field influence. The switch issues a variable strength voltage that turns an electrical CIRCUIT on and off. The Hall-Effect switch was used widely in ignition system DISTRIBUTORs having no CONTACT POINTS.

Halogen Headlamp. A halogen headlamp is a HEADLIGHT case having a small, high-intensity inner bulb filled with halogen to surround the filament. The halogen headlamp is credited with possessing a very high-intensity light.

 When replacing halogen bulbs, care should be taken to avoid touching the bulb. Skin oils will cause the bulb to fail.

Harmonic Balancer. See VIBRATION DAMPER.

Hazard Warning Light. The hazard warning light is a bulb CIRCUIT that can be activated by the driver if the vehicle is stopped or running under hazardous conditions. Used in sets of four—one bulb and its yellow lens for each corner of the vehicle—the hazard warning light circuit is operated by a SWITCH on the STEERING COLUMN. *Also see* TURN SIGNAL *and* BRAKE LIGHT.

Headlamp. The headlamp may also be called a HEADLIGHT. The headlamp is a light or housing in the vehicle front used to illuminate the road during dim light or darkness. Other headlamps remain illuminated during daylight hours to increase driving safety. Some headlamps use sealed beam bulbs. Others headlamps use halogen bulbs.

Headlight. A headlight is a high-intensity bulb or bulb assembly that illuminates the road ahead of the vehicle. *See* HEADLAMP.

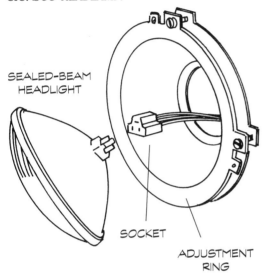

SEALED-BEAM
HEADLIGHT

SOCKET

ADJUSTMENT
RING

Headlight Switch. A headlight switch is a driver operated switch that controls the lighting of the headlights, and often other exterior and interior lights. The switch is mounted on the dashboard in older vehicles, and in the TURN SIGNAL lever of late model vehicles.

Heat Control Valve. The heat control valve is often called the heat riser. The VALVE is located in the EXHAUST MANIFOLD outlet. The heat control valve diverts heat to the INTAKE MANIFOLD to quickly warm it during initial engine starting.

Used mainly with a CARBURETOR or CENTRAL FUEL INJECTION (CFI), the exhaust diversion causes rapid cold weather fuel vaporization. Also called EFE (early fuel evaporation).

Heater. The heater is an air circulation unit designed to deliver warmed outside, ambient air to the interior passenger compartment of the vehicle. The heater can raise the temperature of the incoming air by routing the air, or a portion of the air, through the HEATER CORE. Driven by a blower FAN, the amount of air flowing through the core determines the heater outlet temperature. In our liquid-cooled engines, the core routes the incoming air around its tubes. The tubes are internally heated by the engine COOLANT.

Outside air can also flow through the heater core and be routed by heater control doors to flow through ducts to the base of the windshield. This flow can defog or defrost the windshield during cold and humid vehicle operations.

Heater Control Valve. A heater control valve allows engine COOLANT to flow to the passenger HEATER through heater hoses. If stuck, the unit may cause poor A/C or heater performance. If leaking, the unit may cause coolant loss. If the valve control DIAPHRAGM is ruptured, the ENGINE may ingest coolant into the COMBUSTION CHAMBERS via the valve's VACUUM control circuit.

Heater Core. A heater core is a small heat exchange RADIATOR. The core usually mounts beneath the INSTRUMENT PANEL, usually in the A/C or HEATER plenum housing. Heated COOLANT mixture flows through the core. The core transfers heat to the passenger compartment air as the plenum control doors permit.

Heating Element. A device that provides heat by passing ELECTRIC CURRENT through a high resistance. Used in heated seats.

Heat Sink. A heat sink is a device designed to absorb heat. DIODEs in an ALTERNATOR, for example, generate damaging heat. Diodes are therefore usually heat-sink mounted for cooling.

High-Energy Ignition (HEI). A high-energy ignition system is an electronic IGNITION SYSTEM capable of producing very high SPARK PLUG firing voltages.

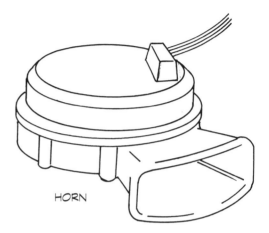

HORN

Horn. In cars, the horn is an electrical sounding device operated via MAGNETISM. The magnet pulses sound vibrations in answer to an electrical RELAY signal. In trucks, the horn may operate using air pressure. In both installations, horns usually mount in pairs and sound a warning when the vehicle operator depresses a button on the STEERING WHEEL.

Horn Relay. The horn relay electrically connects between the BATTERY and the HORN. Pressing a horn button energizes the RELAY. The relay contains CONTACT POINTS that close, connecting the horn to the high current available from the battery.

A horn relay that sticks closed will often cause non-stop horn operation.

Horsepower. Horsepower is a measurement scale for mechanical power. Horsepower states the strength and rate at which work is done. One horsepower is 33,000 ft. lbs. (foot pounds) of work accomplished per minute. The rating compares the power of an ENGINE to that of workhorses.

Hub. The hub is the center portion of a GEAR, WHEEL, or FAN. The hub attaches the device to another mechanical part.

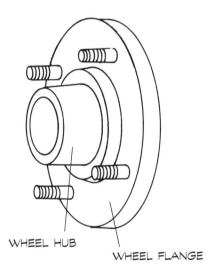

WHEEL HUB

WHEEL FLANGE

Hydraulic or Hydraulics. Pertaining to a fluid or liquid under pressure is the science of hydraulics. The word is derived from the Greek term "hydro," meaning liquid. Liquid under pressure can transmit force or motion, or both.

Hydraulic Brakes. Hydraulic brakes use fluid motion and pressure to force a BRAKE LINING against a BRAKE to stop a vehicle.

Hydraulic Brake Booster. A hydraulic brake booster uses a strong hydraulic pressure to assist driver BRAKE application. The pump may be operated from ENGINE power or electrically driven. Occasionally, the POWER STEERING hydraulic pump doubles as a hydraulic brake booster. The hydraulic brake booster may also be part of the ANTI-LOCK BRAKE SYSTEM (ABS).

Hydraulic Pressure. A measure of force on a liquid. Often measured in value by psi (pounds per square inch) or kg/cm (kilograms per cubic centimeter), hydraulic pressure can provide PISTON motion and apply force.

Hydraulic Valve Lifter. Often called a FOLLOWER, a hydraulic valve lifter uses oil pressure delivered from the ENGINE

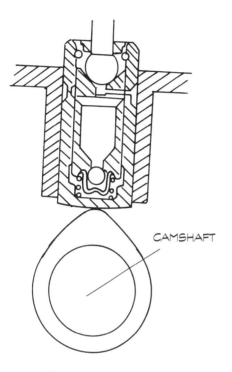

CAMSHAFT

CROSS-SECTION OF
HYDRAULIC VALVE LIFTER

oiling system to keep VALVE operating mechanisms in constant contact with

the CAM LOBES. The lifter design allows changes in VALVETRAIN length to occur due to temperature changes.

Hydrocarbon (HC). A hydrocarbon is a physical compound primarily containing HYDROGEN and CARBON atoms. Hydrocarbons are usually derived from fossil fuels such as coal and petroleum, and natural gases. GASOLINE, DIESEL FUEL, and LIQUID PROPANE GAS (LPG) are blends of hydrocarbons refined from crude oil. Unburned hydrocarbons are agents in the formation of smog pollution.

Hydrogen (H). Hydrogen is an odorless, colorless, highly flammable GAS. The COMBUSTION (rapid oxidation) of hydrogen produces heat and water.

IAC. *See* IDLE AIR CONTROL.

Idle Air Control (IAC). An IAC is the intake air bypass used in a FUEL INJECTION system to control the engine idling speed. Computer activated, the unit may supply extra air during warm-up. This compensates for poor fuel vaporization and thick engine OIL. As well, the IAC often steps-up air flow and engine IDLE SPEED to compensate for accessory load, such as the A/C, POWER STEERING, and high ALTERNATOR load.

Idler Arm. Used in parallelogram STEERING LINKAGE, the idler arm is a link that supports the STEERING ARM end and TIE ROD shaft opposite the steering gearbox.

Idle Solenoid. An idle solenoid (motor) and plunger is used to provide an adjusted throttle setting at idle. Used primarily with a CARBURETOR, the adjusted throttle setting governs the engine IDLE SPEED.

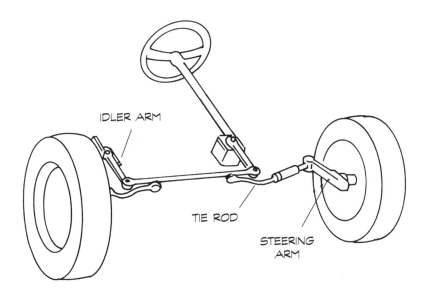

IDLER ARM

TIE ROD

STEERING
ARM

Idle Speed. The idle speed is the revolutions per minute (rpm) speed at which the ENGINE runs when the ACCELERATOR or throttle pedal has not been depressed by the vehicle operator.

Idle Speed Control (ISC). An idle speed control motor is usually an electrical rotary or stepper MOTOR. The unit controls the position of THROTTLE PLATEs of an idling ENGINE within a CARBURETOR or THROTTLE BODY. The ISC's plunger position is usually controlled by computer.

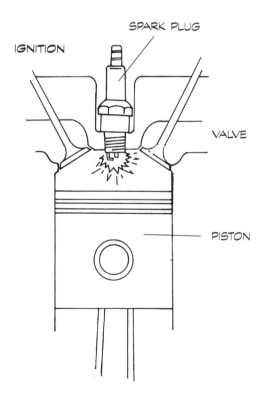

IGNITION

SPARK PLUG

VALVE

PISTON

Ignition. Ignition is the initial FUEL burning created by sufficient heat in an engine CYLINDER. In DIESEL ENGINEs, the heat of COMPRESSION starts the burning. In GAS engines, compression heat raises the cylinder temperature to just below the ignition temperature. Then the SPARK PLUG supplies sufficient heat to fire the air/fuel mixture.

Ignition Analyzer. An ignition analyzer is a test instrument used by repair technicians that displays an IGNITION SYSTEM's electrical information. Used in system diagnosis, the instrument may contain both meter readouts and oscilloscope patterns. The ignition analyzer may be used in conjunction with an EXHAUST ANALYZER and OSCILLOSCOPE.

Ignition Coil. The ignition coil is an electrical transformer that increases BATTERY voltage to several thousand volts to fire an engine's SPARK PLUGs.

Ignition Distributor. An ignition distributor is usually a rotary unit that contains the switching that closes and opens the primary COIL circuit at the proper time for needed IGNITION. The switching may be mechanical or solid-state, depending on the year and model vehicle. The ignition distributor is also so named because it distributes the resulting high-voltage surges from the coil secondary winding, through the distributor ignition ROTOR, to the spark plugs.

Ignition Module. The ignition module is used in an electronic IGNITION SYSTEM to open and close a coil's PRIMARY CIRCUIT. The ignition module may be a separate unit or a portion of the POWERTRAIN CONTROL MODULE function (PCM, ECM, or ECU).

Ignition Resistor. The ignition resistor is a RESISTANCE unit that alters ignition PRIMARY CIRCUIT voltage. The ignition resistor reduces BATTERY voltage at the ignition COIL during engine operation. Used in early point-type IGNITION SYSTEMS, the voltage reduction eliminated most CONTACT POINT erosion and pitting.

A vehicle should not be operated without the ignition resistor. Coil and module failure will result.

Ignition Switch. The ignition switch is a key-operated SWITCH that opens and closes the voltage supply CIRCUIT to the IGNITION and other electrical systems of the automobile. The average modern switch contains OFF/LOCK, ON, START, and ACCESSORY working positions.

Ignition System. The ignition system is the electrical system that furnishes timed, high voltage impulses to the SPARK PLUGS of a SPARK IGNITION ENGINE. The system incorporates adjustment of spark-timing based on engine speed, load, and other factors. *See* IGNITION TIMING.

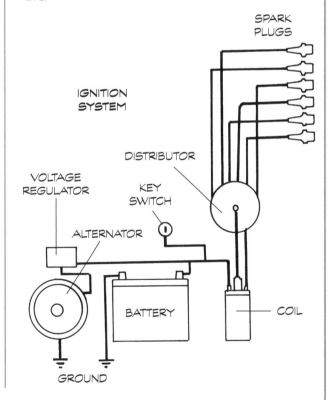

Ignition Timing. The ignition timing controls the firing of the ignition coil SECONDARY CIRCUIT voltage across the air GAP of a SPARK PLUG. The event is timed for proper COMBUSTION occurrence near the juncture of the COMPRESSION STROKE and POWER STROKE. Timing is expressed in degrees relative to PISTON and CRANKSHAFT position; before TOP DEAD CENTER POSITION (BTDC); or after TOP DEAD CENTER (ATDC).

Impeller. An impeller is a fan blade equipped circular structure used to pump a gaseous or liquid material. Looking somewhat fan-like in appearance, impellers are commonly used in WATER PUMPS, TURBOCHARGERS, FLUID COUPLINGS, and TORQUE CONVERTERS.

Included Angle (IA). The included angle (IA) is an operating angle of the front SUSPENSION system. The included angle is composed of the wheel CAMBER angle plus the STEERING AXIS INCLINATION (SAI). Included angle is built into the vehicle suspension geometry and is usually not adjustable. Errors in suspension included angle may indicate bent steering parts.

Induction. Induction is the introducing of potential or material. These include:

■ Electrical induction produces a voltage in a CONDUCTOR or COIL via influence of a magnetic field.

■ Air induction introduces cool ambient air to the engine intake air stream. Therefore the dense, cooler air contains more OXYGEN per cubic foot than heated air, for improved COMBUSTION characteristics.

Inertia. Inertia is the energy of a moving object that causes the object to resist changes in speed or direction of travel. For example, an engine FLYWHEEL stores and releases inertial momentum that smoothes engine power pulses coming from the CYLINDERS.

Input Shaft. An input shaft is a cylindrical object that delivers TORQUE to a mechanical apparatus. The shaft is usually supported by one or more BUSHINGS or BEARINGS that surround the shaft-bearing JOURNAL(s). The shaft may contain surface grooves or drilled passages for lubrication purposes.

Instrument Panel. The instrument panel is the vehicle operator console that contains the gauges, indicators, lights, and information the driver needs to operate the vehicle.

Insulation. Insulation is a material that prevents the travel of heat or electricity.

Intake Air Sensor. *See* AIR FLOW CONTROL.

Intake Air Temperature Sensor (IAT). The intake air temperature sensor is usually a THERMISTOR that samples the intake air as it passes through the engine air intake system. The SENSOR, which may operate in concert with a MASS AIR FLOW (MAF) SENSOR or MANIFOLD ABSOLUTE PRESSURE (MAP) SENSOR, sends voltage information to the FUEL INJECTION control computer. The computer adjusts the air/fuel mixture to compensate for intake air temperature variations. This unit is often called the MANIFOLD AIR TEMPERATURE SENSOR (MATS).

Intake Manifold. The intake manifold is a set of pipes, passages, or tubes through which air or air/fuel mixture flows. The engine intake manifold allows air or air/fuel mixture to flow from the THROTTLE valves to the CYLIN-

DER intake ports. The manifold may also contain passages for the flow of COOLANT, EXHAUST GAS RECIRCULATION (EGR), VACUUM, and heat-riser gases.

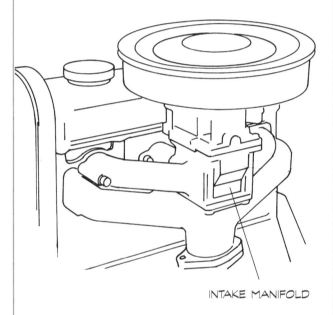

INTAKE MANIFOLD

Intake Stroke. The intake stroke occurs from TOP DEAD CENTER to BOTTOM DEAD CENTER, and is the point during which the INTAKE VALVE becomes wide open. The intake stroke immediately follows the EXHAUST STROKE. Before the intake stroke begins, the intake valve begins to open. The CYLINDER fills with air if it is a DIESEL ENGINE, or an air/fuel mixture if the engine is GASOLINE powered.

Intake Valve. The intake valve is a poppet-style VALVE that admits INTAKE MANIFOLD air or air/fuel mixture into an engine CYLINDER. The valve lifts from its seat during the intake cycle, opened by a CAM LOBE and its attending VALVETRAIN components. The intake valve then closes via spring tension to trap the compressible mass in the cylinder.

Subject to high COMBUSTION heat, improper contact with the VALVE SEAT area may cause intake valve burning. If a portion of the VALVE HEAD burns away, it leaks COMPRESSION back into the intake manifold. As well, subject to excess VALVE GUIDE wear at its stem, the valve can improperly seat and burn. Valve burning usually requires engine disassembly for repairs.

Integrated Circuit. Tiny solid-state electrical circuitry manufactured in controlled conditions is called an integrated circuit. The integrated circuits often contain microchips or chips that are capable of complex electronic circuit functions.

Integrated circuits and chips, because of their size and complexity, offer little or no opportunity for repair. They must be replaced when defective.

Interaxle Differential. *See* CENTER DIFFERENTIAL.

Intercooler. An intercooler is a radiator-like device that cools the compressed air exiting a SUPERCHARGER or TURBOCHARGER before it enters the ENGINE. Sometimes called the AFTERCOOLER, this unit supplies air cooling, which increases air density. Cool, dense air promotes improved FUEL burning and increases engine performance.

ISC. *See* IDLE SPEED CONTROL. *Also see* IAC.

Jack. A jack is the lifting mechanism designed to raise a vehicle or vehicle WHEEL for service.

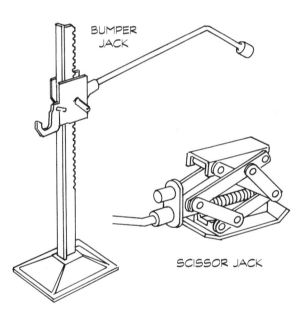

BUMPER JACK

SCISSOR JACK

Always use JACK STANDS when servicing a vehicle. Always jack the vehicle at the recommended JACK POINTS. Check with the vehicle manufacturer or a service technician for service recommendations.

Jacking Points. Places designed to absorb the stress of jacking a vehicle without damage are called jacking points. Most modern vehicle bodies sport four jacking points. These are specified in location by the car maker as where the JACK is placed for changing a flattened or low pressure TIRE.

Always use JACK STANDS when servicing a vehicle. Always jack the vehicle at the recommended jack points. Check with the vehicle manufacturer or a service technician for service recommendations.

Jack Stands. A jack stand is a safety stand designed for use after the vehicle is raised by a JACK.

Jack stands should always be firmly and strategically placed before anyone has access beneath a vehicle. Always use jack stands when servicing a vehicle. Always jack the vehicle at the recommended JACKING

POINTS. Check with the vehicle manufacturer or a service technician for service recommendations.

Jam. A jam is a halting of unit function due to mechanical binding or GEAR mismatch. For example, if the windshield wiper LINKAGE jams with ice obstruction, the wiper blades fail to operate. FUSEs may blow, wiper blades tear, or the wiper MOTOR may burn out from overload.

Jet. *See* NOZZLE

Journal. A journal is the portion of a rotating shaft that revolves in a BEARING.

Jumper Wire. A jumper wire is a wire length used to temporarily connect an ELECTRIC CIRCUIT for diagnostic purposes.

Jump-Starting. Also called jumpering, jump-starting is the process that cranks the ENGINE in a vehicle that has a discharged (dead) BATTERY. Jumpering using jumper cables may be done from a special starting unit or a second battery.

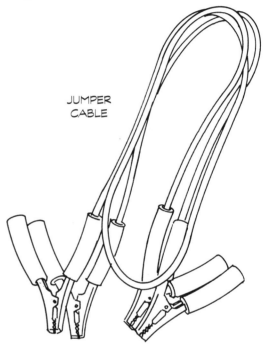

JUMPER CABLE

Because of POLARITY considerations and the possible ignition of HYDROGEN gases, jumpering should only be done by knowledgeable individuals.

Kickdown. Also called the PASSING GEAR, kickdown is a downshift of an AUTOMATIC TRANSMISSION that occurs automatically when the ACCELERATOR PEDAL is pushed close to the passenger compartment floorboard. The downshift provides greater TORQUE, but higher engine speed is required to maintain vehicle speed and acceleration. The kickdown causes the TRANSMISSION to revert to a CLUTCH and/or SERVO and BAND that provided the GEAR on the upshifting sequence.

Kingpin. A kingpin is a cylindrical pin that mounts the front wheel STEERING KNUCKLE to an AXLE. Used in many straight axle SUSPENSIONs found in heavy-duty vehicles, KINGPINs and their BUSHINGs are subject to wear. If wear occurs, camber, caster, and toe errors can occur. *See* CASTER, CAMBER, *and* TOE.

Knock. Knock is a deep, metallic sound emitted from an ENGINE. It is described as:

■ The name given for untimely fuel DETONATION, often called spark knock. This type of knock usually occurs under engine load and diminishes as the THROTTLE setting is lessened. Often the noise is generated by vibrations in the CONNECTING ROD. Continued knocking can cause serious engine damage. *Also see* PING.

■ A sound that varies according to engine speed. The knock is usually caused by a loose PISTON PIN or connecting rod bearing, crankshaft MAIN BEARING, or loose VIBRATION DAMPER torsional ring. A knock that sounds off under power as the engine speed rises may also be caused by excess piston skirt CLEARANCEs.

Knock Sensor. A knock sensor is a piezoelectric SENSOR screwed into the ENGINE to detect the sounds of engine combustion KNOCK. The sensor, detecting a fuel or ignition knock, automatically retards the spark plug TIMING to rid the engine of CYLINDER and PISTON damaging pressure spikes.

Knuckle. The front SUSPENSION component that supports the front WHEEL and permits it to turn and steer the vehicle is called the knuckle. Depending on the year and model, the knuckle pivots on BALL JOINTS, KINGPINS, or MacPherson strut suspension BEARINGs.

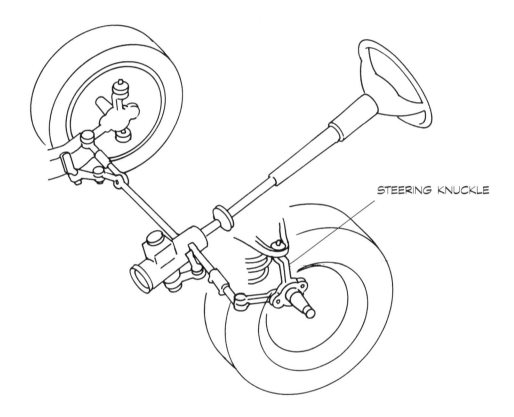

STEERING KNUCKLE

Lash. Lash is the free motion in a mechanical assembly before the load applies. The CLEARANCE provided allows for heat expansion. Lash is found in automobile gear drives or in engine VALVETRAIN. If excessive lash exists, operating noise (clanking or clacking) is usually heard.

 Lash needs to be checked and adjusted on a regular basis. Check with the vehicle manufacturer or a service technician for service recommendations.

Lead. (*pronounced* led) Lead is a heavy metal element that is used in lead-acid storage battery PLATEs.

 To avoid lead pollution, automobile batteries should be serviced and replaced by a qualified technician so that proper discard procedures are observed.

Lead. (*pronounced* leed) A lead is a wire or cable CONDUCTOR that carries electricity. Leads are used by repair technicians for test meter connection and CIRCUIT diagnosis.

Leading Arm. A leading arm is a vehicle suspension STRUT that extends forward of the SUSPENSION part being controlled. One end of the arm attaches to the controlled part, possibly a component such as the THIRD MEMBER rear DIFFERENTIAL assembly, and the other end attaches to the vehicle's FRAME or UNIBODY structure.

Leaf. A leaf is one layer of a leaf SPRING structure. Made of high-tension steel or composite fiber, the leaf clamps to other leaves, combining their flexibility and strength to carry the vehicle weight. Leaf springs usually attach to the vehicle FRAME or BODY using BUSHINGs and SHACKLEs. The shackles allow the change of leaf spring length as the unit flexes. Occasionally, we find a singular leaf may make up the entire leaf spring unit, but use of these singular leaf units is rare.

Leak Detector. A leak detector is a device used to locate air or fluid leaks. A leak detector may be a(n):

■ Engine COMPRESSION loss detector used to find the presence of CARBON DIOXIDE in the engine COOLING SYSTEM.

■ Fluid or device that detects leaks through an opening where air conditioning REFRIGERANT may escape.

■ Audible hearing device used by a technician to detect automotive water leaks into the passenger compartment. Also, some water leaks may be found by gentle applications of a fine powder at door GASKETs.

Lifter. *See* FOLLOWER.

Limited Slip Differential. A limited slip differential is a drive GEAR assembly containing either a cone CLUTCH, a MULTIPLE-DISC CLUTCH, or a FLUID COUPLING. The limited slip differential engages or locks if one driving wheel spins. Also called a non-slip DIFFERENTIAL, its action provides equal power to both AXLE SHAFTs and DRIVE WHEELS. The unit, however, allows slipping for turns.

Care must be taken when operating a vehicle with limited slip. When one wheel loses traction, both wheels may slip and the vehicle's directional control suffers. Also called POSITRACTION, Sure-Grip, Traction-Lock, Dual-Grip, or a VISCOUS CLUTCH.

Linkage. Linkage is a system of rods, mechanical links or levers which transmit motion.

Liquid Propane Gas. Also known as LPG or propane, liquid propane gas is an alternate FUEL for internal combustion engines. Having differing burning, pollution, and handling characteristics than liquid GASOLINE, LPG finds use in fleet vehicles. It requires very strict fire prevention during FUEL TANK filling due to its high volatility. It is especially suited, however, for use in SPARK IGNITION ENGINEs that operate indoors, such as engines in industrial lift trucks. This is due to very clean LPG fuel and engine exhaust properties.

Locking Hubs. Wheel hubs that can engage or disengage are called locking hubs. Either operated manually or automatically, they often switch the operation of 4WD (FOUR-WHEEL DRIVE) vehicles between 2WD and 4WD. Disengagement of front WHEELs from the front 4WD DIFFERENTIAL and DRIVESHAFT often promotes good FUEL economy and reduced component wear.

Locking Torque Converter. A locking torque converter is an automatic transmission TORQUE CONVERTER that mechanically locks the IMPELLER fan to the output TURBINE via the TORQUE CONVERTER CLUTCH (TCC). This action eliminates natural slippage created by driving the turbine via the TRANSMISSION fluid hydrodynamics.

Longitudinal Arm. A suspension STRUT or ARM that extends forward or backward within the vehicle is called a longitudinal arm. The arm is used in UNIBODY or body-over-frame vehicles to control SUSPENSION component motion. The arm attaches through a BUSHING to the suspension components at one end, and the vehicle body or FRAME at the other. *Also see* LEADING ARM *and* TRAILING ARM.

LPG. *See* LIQUID PROPANE GAS.

Lubrication System. The lubrication system supplies OIL to moving mechanical parts. Consisting of an OIL PUMP, OIL FILTER, and the associated distribution circuits, the lubrication system is designed to prevent or lower frictional contact between moving metal surfaces in the ENGINE.

Machine. The machine is a unit that produces power by the conversion of energy. The automobile ENGINE is a machine. As a verb, to machine is to use cutting or refinishing tools to finish or refinish such items as BRAKE DRUMS, brake ROTORS, FLYWHEELS, a CYLINDER HEAD, or an ENGINE BLOCK.

MacPherson Strut Suspension. A MacPherson strut suspension is a vehicle SUSPENSION system that combines the COIL SPRING and SHOCK ABSORBER into a single, unitized assembly. The MacPherson strut nests into an underhood strut tower at the top, pivoting on a rotary BEARING. The tower and bearing therefore carry the vehicle weight. The strut fastens to a lower CONTROL ARM at the strut bottom end via its KNUCKLE and a BALLJOINT. The lower control arm and LONGITUDINAL ARM (LEADING ARM or TRAILING ARM) thus connect the strut assembly to the lower vehicle body.

Used in modern automobiles, MacPherson strut suspension saves vehicle weight and improves economy. Strut design, however, offers little opportunity for dynamic front geometry changes in caster and camber while the vehicle is in motion. These dimensions are built into the strut and its mountings as fixed running dimensions. Alignment adjustments may be made to a vehicle by changes in strut

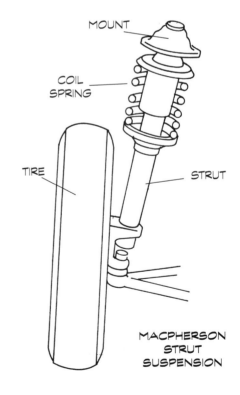

MACPHERSON
STRUT
SUSPENSION

camber, control arm, and longitudinal arm or strut lengths. *Also see* CASTER, CAMBER, CONTROL ARM, *and* STRUT.

Magnetic Clutch. A magnetic clutch is used to engage and disengage a vehicle air conditioning COMPRESSOR or other devices. Using an ELECTROMAGNETIC field, the magnet energizes to push or pull the PLATE into contact with a PRESSURE PLATE.

Magnetic Force. Magnetic force is the field of magnetic influence surrounding a magnet or electromagnet. Magnetic force is expressed schematically by dotted lines.

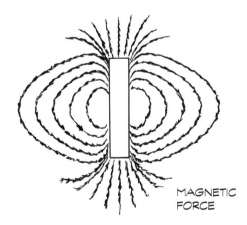

MAGNETIC FORCE

Magnetic Induction. Magnetic induction is the condition that allows a voltage to be induced in a COIL by a changing magnetic field. The success rate of the induced voltage depends on the comparative number of turns in the two coils and the distance between the coils.

Magnetic Switch. A magnetic switch has an ELECTROMAGNETIC winding that causes the switch contacts to open or close an electrical circuit or circuits.

Magnetism. Magnetism is the ability to attract iron.

Main Bearing. The main bearing in the ENGINE encases a crankshaft's main JOURNAL. The main bearing is usually a soft metal insert manufactured to close tolerances that sits in a saddle in the ENGINE BLOCK. The main bearing only allows sufficient CLEARANCE for a cooling, cushioning, and lubricating OIL film presence.

🚌 Dirty engine oil often leads to main bearing damage that can shorten an engine service life.

Malfunction Indicator Light (MIL). The malfunction indicator light illuminates in the INSTRUMENT PANEL to warn the vehicle operator of malfunctions that can hamper vehicle operation.

A warning should always be investigated by a qualified technician familiar with OBD and OBD2 operations. If the MIL is flashing, engine operation should be immediately halted to avoid major damage.

Manifold. A manifold has inlet and outlet passageways through which a GAS or liquid distributes. *See* INTAKE MANIFOLD *and* EXHAUST MANIFOLD.

Manifold Absolute Pressure (MAP) Sensor. The MAP is an electrical SENSOR that measures the absolute pressure (VACUUM) within the INTAKE MANIFOLD. In this way the sensor detects how much load the ENGINE is under. The MAP sends the measurement signal to the ECM or PCM. The module uses this information to compute the FUEL amounts needed.

Manifold Air Temperature Sensor (MATS). *See* INTAKE AIR TEMPERATURE SENSOR (IAT).

Manifold Gauge. A manifold gauge is a high-pressure and a low-pressure gauge set used for testing pressures in the air conditioning REFRIGERANT system. Also, a manifold gauge is a gauge that senses engine intake manifold VACUUM.

Manifold Pressure. Pressure in the engine INTAKE MANIFOLD is often termed as manifold pressure. If the pressure is above absolute zero but below atmospheric pressure (14.5 psi), automobile repair technicians call this low pressure an ENGINE VACUUM. Pressure levels above atmospheric pressure, usually supplied by supercharging or turbocharging, is called BOOST.

Manifold Sensor. *See* MAP SENSOR.

Manifold Vacuum. MANIFOLD PRESSURE in the INTAKE MANIFOLD that falls below atmospheric pressure (14.5 psi).

Manual Transmission. The manual transmission is a GEAR selection unit that enables the driver to manually match the engine power and speed to the power and speed needs. Gear changes are made manually through a shift LINKAGE assembly, either mounted on the vehicle floor or the STEERING COLUMN. A manual transmission may provide three forward speeds, or up to six speeds. As well, the driver can select a reverse gear linkage position to back the vehicle. Manual transmissions are usually mated with a CLUTCH, depending on the vehicle design. Manual transmissions contain gears and mating SYNCHRONIZERS. The unit carries a level of gear lubricant to reduce frictional heat and wear.

The gear lube level should be checked at every vehicle lubrication servicing.

Manual Valve. The manual valve is a cylindrical SPOOL VALVE that selects the shift range in an AUTOMATIC TRANSMISSION. The manual valve allows HYDRAULIC PRESSURE within the TRANSMISSION to operate CLUTCHes and holding BANDs as selected by the driver.

MAP Sensor. *See* MANIFOLD ABSOLUTE PRESSURE (MAP) SENSOR. This unit may also be called the VACUUM SENSOR or MANIFOLD SENSOR. A MAP sensor usually supplies MANIFOLD PRESSURE information to an engine control computer.

Mass Air Flow Sensor (MAF). A mass air flow sensor is an intake air sensor that measures the amount of air by mass flowing into the engine INTAKE MANIFOLD. *Also see* AIR FLOW CONTROL.

Master Cylinder. The master cylinder is a piston-equipped CYLINDER in a CLUTCH or in HYDRAULIC BRAKES. Filled with hydraulic fluid, the cylinder transmits pressure as the driver depresses the cylinder PISTON and its apply rod using a BRAKE PEDAL. The modern dual master cylinder has two brake apply circuits that apply diagonal brake circuits.

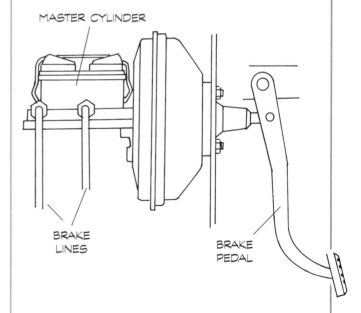

MASTER CYLINDER

BRAKE LINES

BRAKE PEDAL

Mesh. The smooth engaging of gear

teeth is called a mesh. Smooth GEAR meshing is usually assisted using gear speed SYNCHRONIZERS and proper lubrication.

Metering Rod. A metering rod is a small movable or step-shaped rod in a CARBURETOR. The rod, centered in a JET, increases or decreases FUEL flow according to engine THROTTLE opening, load, or both.

Metering Valve. A metering valve is a hydraulic control VALVE in the DISC BRAKE system that prevents pressure build-up in the front BRAKES until after the rear brakes are applied. The valve action helps the rear wheels stabilize vehicle direction during stops.

Methanol. Wood or methyl alcohol. Methanol is an alternate FUEL for SPARK IGNITION ENGINES.

Microprocessor. A microprocessor is a small SOLID-STATE electronic computer unit. SENSORS and SWITCHes provide input that the microprocessor uses for output calculations.

MIL. *See* MALFUNCTION INDICATOR LIGHT.

Mixture Control Solenoid (M/C Solenoid). The mixture control solenoid is part of the FEEDBACK CARBURETOR which varies the amount of FUEL the ENGINE receives based on signals from the POWERTRAIN CONTROL MODULE (PCM).

Modulator Valve. A modulator valve is used in an AUTOMATIC TRANSMISSION to operate the TRANSMISSION using engine intake manifold VACUUM. Through the VALVE, the vacuum signal changes transmission HYDRAULIC PRESSUREs in response to changes in engine load. The modulator valve is activated by a unit called the VACUUM MODULATOR CANISTER.

Motor. An energy conversion device, a motor is:

■ A slang expression for an ENGINE that converts the chemical energy from FUEL into mechanical energy. Scientifically called a "prime mover," a motor is more correctly referred to as an engine in the automobile industry.

■ A device that converts electrical energy into mechanical energy. For example, the STARTER MOTOR, or the power window motor are examples of motors.

Muffler. A muffler is a baffled or chambered device in the engine EXHAUST SYSTEM. The internal baffles or chambers dampen the EXHAUST pulses and reduce the exhaust noise as the exhaust flows through the unit. The muffler is performance matched (tuned) to provide quiet operation, yet create low exhaust system back pressures on ENGINE breathing.

Also, used in AIR CONDITIONING SYSTEMS, a muffler unit may be present to minimize noisy pumping sounds emitted from the COMPRESSOR.

Multiple Disc Clutch. A multiple disc clutch has more than one FRICTION DISC. Used predominately in the AUTOMATIC TRANSMISSION, the CLUTCH unit contains several driving discs and mating DRIVEN DISCS that are alternately placed. The discs are wet-clutch design, meaning they are lubricated by the TRANSMISSION fluid.

Multiple (Multi) Viscosity Oil. Engine oil that exhibits a lower VISCOSITY (liquid thickness) when cold and a higher viscosity when hot is called a multiple (multi) viscosity oil. The multiplicity of viscosity character aids cold starting.

Multipoint Fuel Injection (MFI or MPFI). *See* PORT FUEL INJECTION.

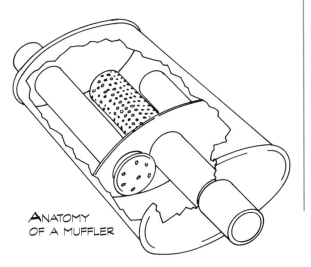

ANATOMY
OF A MUFFLER

Negative. Negative is one of the two poles of a magnet. Also, negative is one of the two terminals of a complete DIRECT CURRENT electrical CIRCUIT. The other terminal is called the POSITIVE terminal. The negative terminal on a vehicle BATTERY is usually identified as the battery post having the smallest diameter. The minus sign (–) located on the terminal is normally used to help identify the negative pole. On most automobiles, the negative terminal is also the electrical GROUND terminal. Jumper

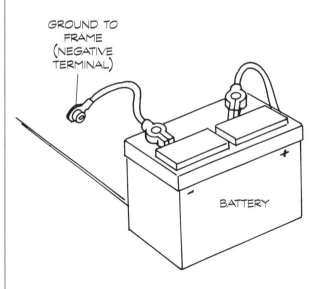

GROUND TO
FRAME
(NEGATIVE
TERMINAL)

BATTERY

cables are often connected to the terminals to start a vehicle with a deficient battery charge.

⚠ To help avoid dangerous sparking during starting CABLE connections, the negative cable is connected after the positive cable, and disconnected last.

🚌 Battery cable connections should be cleaned during vehicle maintenance to ensure good electrical continuity.

Neutral. The setting of a TRANSMISSION function wherein all GEARs are disengaged is called neutral. In neutral, the OUTPUT SHAFT is disconnected from the INPUT SHAFT. In an AUTOMATIC TRANSMISSION, park is also a neutral range having the addition of a DRIVELINE locking function. *See* PARK.

Neutral Start Switch. Used as a safety device, the neutral start switch is wired into the STARTER circuit. The SWITCH prevents engine cranking until the TRANSMISSION linkage is placed in the PARK or NEUTRAL position.

Nitrogen Oxides (NOx). Chemical compounds of NITROGEN and OXYGEN are called nitrogen oxides. The mix is a basic air pollutant that helps to form smog. Automotive emission levels of NOx are limited by law. NOx is also referred to as oxides of nitrogen.

North Pole. The polarity from which MAGNETIC FORCE leaves a magnet.

Nozzle. A pressure or flow control opening through which a GAS or liquid passes. Often called a JET or ORIFICE.

Octane Rating. The octane rating is a measure of the burning properties of a GASOLINE. The higher the rating number, the slower the FUEL burns. Also, the higher the rating number the less spark KNOCK or DETONATION tendency a gasoline contains. High-performance, high-compression engines may require high octane rated gasoline.

ODB or OBD2. *See* ON-BOARD DIAGNOSTICS.

Odometer. An odometer is an INSTRUMENT PANEL display that tallies the distance the vehicle has traveled. In today's vehicle, the odometer may be either an ANALOG GAUGE or DIGITAL METER.

⚠ It is illegal to tamper with an odometer reading.

Ohm. The ohm is a unit of electric resistance related to voltage and amperage. Ohm's Law states that a volt will force one ampere of current through one ohm of RESISTANCE. *Also see* VOLT *and* AMPERE.

Ohmmeter. An ohmmeter is an electrical meter designed to measure the RESISTANCE of an electrical CIRCUIT. Resistance is measured in OHMS. The meter connects in series with the electrical circuit to be measured. An ohmmeter may be a part of the function of a multimeter, which also measures a circuit's voltage and amps.

Oil. Petroleum oil is a liquid HYDROCARBON used for the production of FUEL and

lubrication products. Often called crude oil, the liquid oil stock is chemically distilled and fractured into various fuels. Heavy hydrocarbon oils, often called bunker oils, are used as fuel for large industrial or ship engines. Heavy oils are also used for GREASE, GEAR, or MACHINE lubricants. Lighter oils are used as stock for heating oil, kerosene, DIESEL FUEL, and GASOLINE. The vapors of the distilling process siphon into light gases such as natural gas and propane. Used as ENGINE oils, light oils are graded into VISCOSITY (thickness) ratings. Various additives suit the oil for the service recommended. Oil does not wear out. It breaks down into other lighter hydrocarbons, contaminates, or loses its additives. In contrast, synthetic (non-petroleum) oils usually contain lower hydrocarbon levels, and SYNTHETIC OILs are specifically manufactured for various applications.

See OIL FILTER.

Replace engine oil within the vehicle manufacturer recommendations or the intervals specified by the oil manufacturer.

Oil Clearance. Oil clearance is the space between the BEARING and the shaft rotating within it. Excess clearance lowers lubrication retention and often causes a KNOCK or rattle of the shaft within the bearing. Insufficient clearance can cause poor cushioning and bearing failure results.

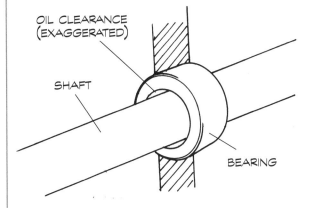

Oil Cooler. An oil cooler is a small radiator-like heat exchanger used to lower the temperature of OIL flowing through it. An oil cooler is often used with a heavy-duty ENGINE or TRANSMISSION application.

Oil Dipstick. An oil dipstick is an OIL level indicator found in most ENGINE installations. The dipstick is a graduated rod that extends into the engine OIL PAN to measure the amount of oil available for engine lubrication. Sometimes the dipstick is augmented by an oil level SENSOR in the reservoir that turns on an INSTRUMENT PANEL warning light if the oil level is low.

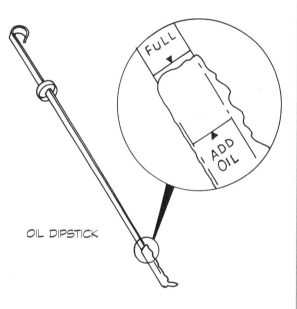

OIL DIPSTICK

Oil level should be checked at every gas fill-up. Check with the vehicle manufacturer or a service technician for service recommendations.

Oil Filter. An oil filter removes solid impurities from the engine OIL. The oil passes through a FILTER medium that allows only cleaned oil to flow through. If a filter becomes overloaded, often a bypass allows continued lubrication,

but with dirty oil. Rated according to their micron level of filtration, even quality filters need service at recommended intervals.

Check with the vehicle or filter manufacturer, or a competent automobile technician for service interval recommendations.

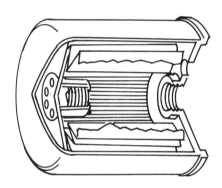

CUTAWAY OF AN OIL FILTER

Oil Pan. The oil pan is a removable lower cover or reservoir that encloses the CRANKCASE. The oil pan holds the OIL in reserve. The pan provides a drawing point for the engine OIL PUMP and a drain catch area for oil returning from the engine parts and the LUBRICATION SYSTEM. During engine repairs, the oil pan is often removed to gain access to the oil pump, CRANKSHAFT, crankshaft

MAIN BEARINGS, CONNECTING RODS, and rod bearings.

Oil Pressure Indicator/Gauge. An oil pressure indicator or gauge mounts in the INSTRUMENT PANEL to indicate engine OIL pressure information. If displayed by a light, the indicator illuminates if the oil pressure falls too low. If an electrical ANALOG GAUGE, graphic bar, number, or pointer display, the gauge indicates the amount of engine oil pressure present.

⚠ If warning is given by an oil pressure indicator or gauge, the engine operation should be immediately halted.

Oil Pressure Sensor. An oil pressure sensor connects to the engine oil pressure CIRCUIT to monitor the available engine oil pressure. If oil pressure falls to an inadequate level, the indicator system provides the driver with warning.

Oil Pump. An oil pump is usually a gear-driven pump housed in or on the ENGINE, or engine OIL PAN reservoir. The oil pump is the LUBRICATION SYSTEM device that forces OIL from the oil pan reservoir to the moving engine parts. If oil pressure falls too low at an engine idle, or causes a warning light blinking at engine idle, the oil pump may be excessively worn or have its intake screen clogged. An oil pump that has completely failed causes a complete loss of oil pressure. In this case, engine damage usually results from continued engine operation.

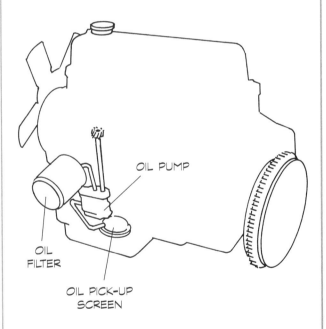

OIL PUMP

OIL FILTER

OIL PICK-UP SCREEN

On-Board Diagnostics (OBD) or (OBD2). On-board diagnostics offers INSTRUMENT PANEL or tester readings of information and TROUBLE CODES that can guide a technician in diagnostic troubleshooting. The trained technician can translate the information or codes into guidance for vehicle repairs. The ODB system also monitors EMISSION CONTROL components and signals the driver if any faults are indicated.

One-Way Clutch. *See* SPRAG CLUTCH.

Open Circuit. An open circuit is a term used to describe an electric CIRCUIT having a break or opening. Sometimes called an open continuity, the opening prevents the passage of electrical current through the circuit.

Open Loop. Open loop is a period of ENGINE operation where the air/fuel mixture is based on pre-programmed instructions and is not modified by the feedback system. Open loop occurs, for example, when the engine is first started, and needs a rich air/fuel mixture for warm-up or at WIDE-OPEN-THROTTLE (WOT) conditions. CLOSED LOOP air/fuel mixture control is suspended during this period.

Optical. An optical device measures, or uses, light. An optical SENSOR, used in some IGNITION SYSTEMS to detect ENGINE firing position, detects the existence of light passing through shutters on an ignition DISTRIBUTOR shaft. *See* PHOTODIODE.

Orifice. An orifice is a small hole, cavity, or passage. Used for fluid pressure control in AUTOMATIC TRANSMISSIONS, for example, an orifice often tailors and times the application and release of a hydraulic SERVO or CLUTCH. *See* NOZZLE *and* JET.

Orifice Tube. An orifice tube is a tube containing a restriction that acts as a flow control in the REFRIGERANT line of an AIR CONDITIONING SYSTEM. The orifice tube metering allows the EVAPORATOR to maintain cool temperatures in the automobile interior.

🚙 Warm air conditioner vent temperatures and rapid COMPRESSOR CLUTCH cycling may be a sign of orifice tube clogging.

O-Ring. An O-ring is a sealing ring made of a rubber or synthetic rubber material. O-rings seal fluid or vapor through COMPRESSION by mechanical action or by system pressure. An O-ring may be used in multiple sets with other rings.

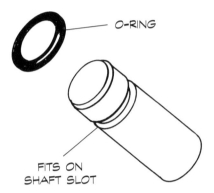

O-RING

FITS ON
SHAFT SLOT

Oscilloscope. An oscilloscope is a visual high-speed VOLTMETER that displays voltage variations via a lighted trace across a television-style picture tube. The tube is called a cathode-ray tube (CRT) display. In modern hand-held instruments, the CRT is replaced by a digital screen similar to that of a portable computer.

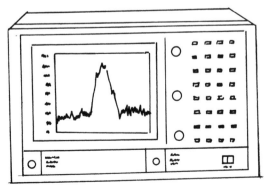

OSCILLOSCOPE

Output Shaft. The TRANSMISSION shaft that delivers the TORQUE from the transmission to the DRIVESHAFT. The output shaft is internally driven by GEARs or a gear-set.

Output Shaft Speed Sensor (OSS). The OSS senses vehicle speed through the OUTPUT SHAFT speed. This information can influence AUTOMATIC TRANSMISSION shifting, CRUISE CONTROL operations, and other POWERTRAIN CONTROL MODULE operations.

Overdrive. A transmission GEAR RATIO that causes the OUTPUT SHAFT to rotate faster than the INPUT SHAFT. Used in the modern automobile, overdrive usually provides a slowing of engine revolutions at high vehicle speed. The gearing provides sufficient power to maintain the speed at high FUEL economy rates, until additional power is needed for climbing a grade.

Overhead Cam (OHC). An overhead CAM is an engine CYLINDER HEAD design that contains the CAMSHAFT. Used in many modern engines, OHC saves fuel energy by eliminating many reciprocating engine parts found in the OVERHEAD

VALVE engine having the camshaft rotating in the ENGINE BLOCK. Overhead cam engines, however, usually have lengthy and elaborate camshaft drive mechanisms.

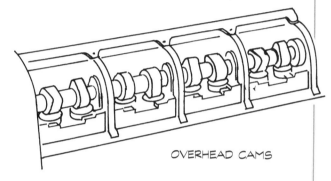

OVERHEAD CAMS

Overhead Valve (OHV). An overhead valve engine is a design in which the VALVEs mount in the CYLINDER HEAD. Located above the COMBUSTION CHAMBER, the poppet-style valves are operated either by LIFTERS, PUSHRODS, and ROCKER ARMS, or by an OVERHEAD CAM. *See* OVERHEAD CAM (OHC).

Over-Running Clutch. An over-running clutch is a mechanical roller or SPRAG CLUTCH that transmits power in only one rotational direction. The unit allows freewheeling in the opposite direction.

■ The over-running clutch is used as a gear's driving or holding mechanism in AUTOMATIC TRANSMISSIONs or the torque converter STATOR.

■ The over-running clutch is sometimes also called the BENDIX in a STARTER MOTOR. The unit allows the starter drive to disengage as the engine CYLINDERs fire. The clutch freewheels as the cylinder power output takes over engine rotation.

Oxygen (O). An odorless, colorless GAS that supports respiration and COMBUSTION. About 20 percent of the air we breathe is oxygen.

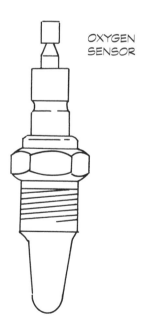

OXYGEN SENSOR

Oxygen (O$_2$) Sensor. The oxygen (O$_2$) sensor samples the exhaust flow as it passes from the engine CYLINDERS though the EXHAUST SYSTEM. The SENSOR generates a voltage dependent on the exhaust stream oxygen content. The voltage signal influences the computations of the fuel injection or carburetion mixture control computer. Oxygen sensors are also used to monitor CATALYTIC CONVERTER efficiency.

A vehicle may be equipped with more than one O$_2$ sensor. These must be replaced at regular service intervals or when the signal becomes unreliable.

Parallel Circuit. A parallel circuit is an electric CIRCUIT wherein two or more electric devices have their terminals sequentially connected together, POSITIVE to positive and NEGATIVE to negative. Each unit operates independently of the other from the same power source. If the RESISTANCE changes in a portion of the circuit, however, due to a burnout and open circuit, current flow through the remaining branches increases. Therefore, the current flow increase could cause burning, and openings also may occur in the remaining branches.

Park. Park is an operational selection for the AUTOMATIC TRANSMISSION. Park usually provides CLUTCH and BAND operations similar to, or the same as, NEUTRAL. Park shifter position, however, usually adds the engagement of the parking pawl that locks transmission OUTPUT SHAFT motion. *See* PAWL.

Parking Brake. A parking brake is a mechanical BRAKE, either foot pedal or hand operated, that is independent of the hydraulic service brakes of the vehicle. Often termed the "emergency brake," the parking brake is set when

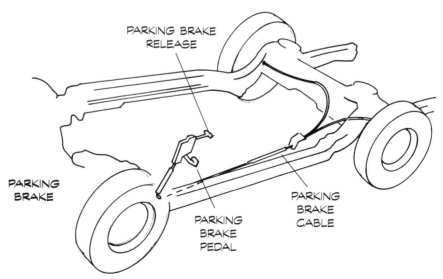

PARKING BRAKE RELEASE

PARKING BRAKE

PARKING BRAKE PEDAL

PARKING BRAKE CABLE

the vehicle is parked. The brake may simply slow or hold the vehicle against rolling in emergency situations. Usually operating at only two of the vehicle's WHEELs, the parking brake is not designed for routine braking duty.

Parking Light. Parking lights are located at the vehicle front to illuminate the vehicle for parking during times of poor visibility. The parking light may be part of the front TURN SIGNAL assembly and bulb, finding independent operation of the dual-element light bulb.

Passing Gear. *See* KICKDOWN.

Passive Restraint. A passive restraint provides vehicle occupant protection during a collision, without requiring any action by the driver or passengers. *See* AIR BAG.

Pawl. A pawl is a catch arm that pivots so that its free end fits into a slot, groove, or detent area. The pawl anchors the held part stationary. Used in the AUTOMATIC TRANSMISSION to hold the vehicle motionless while the shifter is in the PARK range position, the pawl also finds use in windshield wiper

motors, to park the wiper arm blades to the base of the windshield.

PCM. *See* POWERTRAIN CONTROL MODULE.

PCV. *See* POSITIVE CRANKCASE VENTILATION.

Pedal Reserve. Pedal reserve is the measured distance that exists from the BRAKE PEDAL to the floor when the vehicle service BRAKEs are applied.

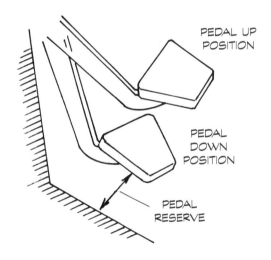

PEDAL UP POSITION

PEDAL DOWN POSITION

PEDAL RESERVE

PFI. *See* PORT FUEL INJECTION.

Photodiode. A photodiode is an electrical current control that uses the presence or absence of light to switch an applied voltage on and off.

Photovoltaic Cell. A photovoltaic cell is a semiconductor unit that generates a DIRECT CURRENT potential (voltage) when it is exposed to light. The photovoltaic unit may also be called a SOLAR CELL.

Pickup Coil. Used in electronic IGNITION SYSTEMS, the pickup coil produces a voltage signal in response to a nearby moving metal mass. The voltage is induced by the moving lumps or teeth on a FLYWHEEL, RELUCTOR, or ARMATURE.

Pilot Bearing. A pilot bearing is a small bearing located in the center of a rotating shaft, to allow differing speeds and centering to occur between the shaft and mating parts. For example, the engine CRANKSHAFT output end carries a pilot bearing. The bearing mates the crankshaft center to the transmission INPUT SHAFT. Defective pilot bearings cause difficult shifting.

 The pilot bearing is usually replaced during clutch service.

Ping. Ping is an engine COMBUSTION noise that occurs during vehicle operation under a load or acceleration. Ping can be caused by SPARK PLUG firings that occur too far in advance. Ping also occurs with FUEL having a too low OCTANE RATING or in engine overheating. The ping noise is usually caused by CONNECTING ROD vibrations.

Pinion Gear. A pinion is the smallest of meshing GEARS. In a drive DIFFERENTIAL, for example, a small pinion gear drives a large diameter RING GEAR to move the automobile.

Piston. A piston is a movable part, usually made of lightweight cast or forged aluminum, that fits snugly into a CYLINDER. The piston receives or transmits motion as a result of pressure changes in a fluid or vapor. In the ENGINE, the piston slides up and down in the cylinder. The piston and its CONNECTING ROD push a ROD BEARING and its JOURNAL to rotate the CRANKSHAFT on MAIN BEARINGS.

Piston Clearance. Piston clearance is the distance allowed between a PISTON and its CYLINDER wall. In an ENGINE, piston clearances are closely controlled at manufacture to allow piston expansion caused by engine operating heat. Excessive CLEARANCE may cause a

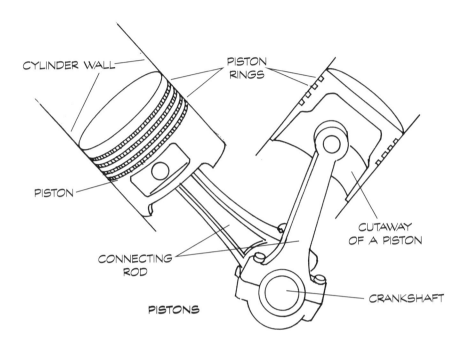

CYLINDER WALL

PISTON RINGS

PISTON

CONNECTING ROD

PISTONS

CUTAWAY OF A PISTON

CRANKSHAFT

knocking noise under power called "piston slap."

Insufficient clearance caused by severe engine overheating may cause seizure.

Piston Displacement. Piston displacement is the air volume displaced during one PISTON upstroke. The ENGINE displacement is the total air pumping volume of all engine CYLINDERS.

Piston Engine. A piston engine uses force applied to reciprocating PISTONS to deliver motive power. Most automotive engines are piston engine design.

Piston Pin. A piston pin is a tubular metal part attaching a PISTON to its CONNECTING ROD. In engines, the piston pin is also termed as the WRIST PIN.

If excess piston pin CLEARANCEs exist, it usually causes a double knocking sound that has rhythm according to engine speed.

Piston Rings. Piston rings are sealing rings fitted into grooves machined into a PISTON. Mounted in an engine piston, compression rings seal the COMPRESSION and COMBUSTION pressures of the COMBUSTION CHAMBER. Engine pistons also have oil rings and their expanders that scrape excess OIL from the CYLINDER wall.

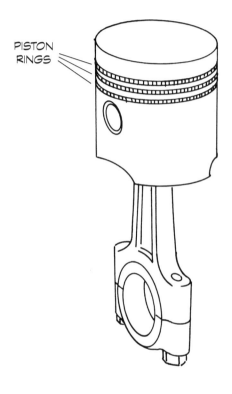

PISTON RINGS

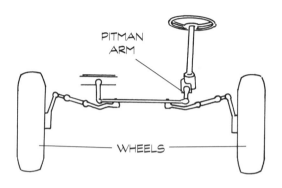

PITMAN ARM

WHEELS

motion. Pitman arms are not a part of RACK AND PINION STEERING.

Wear of the Pitman BUSHING or BEARING can cause steering wander and excess steering wheel play.

Pivot. A pivot is a centering device, pin, BEARING, or shaft upon which another part rotates.

Planetary Gear. A planetary gear rotates around a central sun gear. Often termed as pinions, bearing mounted planetary gears continually MESH between a sun gear an outer ring gear (or internal GEAR). Three or more planets, a sun gear, and a ring gear make up a planetary gear set. Several of these devices may be used in an AUTOMATIC

Failure of the ring SEALs may cause poor engine performance and/or oil consumption.

Pitman Arm. The Pitman arm connects the STEERING BOX output (Pitman) shaft to the STEERING LINKAGE. As the shaft turns, the Pitman arm swings laterally. The motion transfers Pitman shaft movement into steering linkage

TRANSMISSION or 4WD TRANSFER CASE. *See* SUN GEAR *and* RING GEAR.

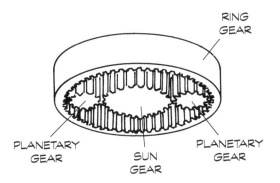

Planet Carrier. A planet carrier is the support or bracket that holds or rotates the axles of PLANETARY GEARs. The carrier may drive the planets or hold them stationary, depending on the CLUTCH or holding BAND applications within the TRANSMISSION.

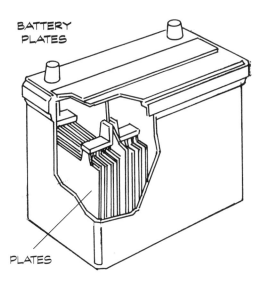

Plate. A plate, as a term used by the auto technician, is a rectangular sheet of spongy lead found in a wet-cell BATTERY. SULFURIC ACID and water in the ELECTROLYTE fluid chemically reacts with the plate lead to store or produce ELECTRON flow.

Play. Play is a term that describes working CLEARANCEs built into a moving part for heat expansion or lubrication. Play that is insufficient invites binding or seizure. Play that is excessive causes greater looseness, operating noise, and wear.

Plies. Plies are the layers of material or cord in the structural casing of a TIRE, a convertible top, or other fabric.

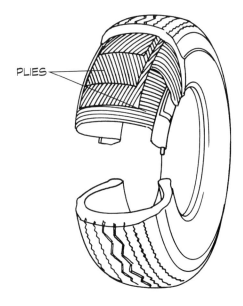

Polarity. The electric charge differences within an electrical CIRCUIT or component that determines current flow is called its polarity.

Port. A port is a passage for the flow of vapor or fluid. A port may be opened and closed by a VALVE, such as the ports within an engine CYLINDER.

Ported Vacuum Switch (PVS). A PVS is a routing device used to switch CARBURETOR ported VACUUM through to such items as the IGNITION VACUUM ADVANCE. Ported vacuum arrives available as the THROTTLE PLATES open slightly. Ported vacuum is used for ignition SPARK PLUG timing modifications, but only during certain periods of engine operation. When the ADVANCE would cause periods of high air pollution, the SWITCH discontinues the vacuum signal operation.

A defective switch may cause increased pollution or improper engine performance.

Port Fuel Injection (PFI). Port fuel injection (PFI) is a FUEL INJECTION system having the fuel injection nozzles positioned to spray FUEL at the INTAKE VALVE head. The injection NOZZLE sprays the fuel charge into the CYLINDER's intake air as the air approaches the intake valve PORT. Also termed MULTIPOINT or MULTIPORT FUEL INJECTION (MFI OR MPFI).

Positive. One of the two poles of a magnet is called positive. Also, one of the two terminals of a complete DIRECT CURRENT electrical CIRCUIT is termed as positive—the other terminal is called the negative terminal. The positive terminal on a BATTERY is usually identified as the battery post having the largest diameter. The plus sign (+) located on the terminal is normally used to help identify the positive pole. *Also see* NEGATIVE.

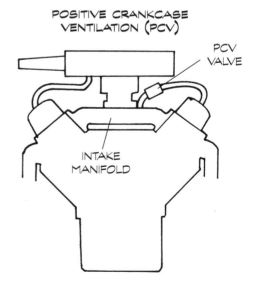

POSITIVE CRANKCASE
VENTILATION (PCV)

PCV
VALVE

INTAKE
MANIFOLD

Positive Crankcase Ventilation (PCV). Positive crankcase ventilation is a ventilation system using intake manifold VACUUM to prevent CRANKCASE EMISSIONS from escaping into the atmosphere. The action routes CRANKCASE vapors and gases to the INTAKE MANIFOLD to be burned. PCV flow is controlled by the PCV valve.

The PCV valve should be serviced according to car manufacturer's recommendations.

Positraction. *See* LIMITED SLIP DIFFERENTIAL.

Power Brake. A power brake system uses HYDRAULIC PRESSURE or ENGINE VACUUM to help a driver provide force required for braking. The BRAKE PEDAL activates both the hydraulic apply pressures and the assist mechanism. The power brake assist valves control the application of assist brake pressure to the hydraulic brake apply circuits. The total result is that less pedal force applies greater stopping fluid pressures in the BRAKE circuit.

Problems that commonly occur in the vacuum type involve loss of engine VACUUM, control valve malfunctions, or brake booster DIAPHRAGM rupture. In the

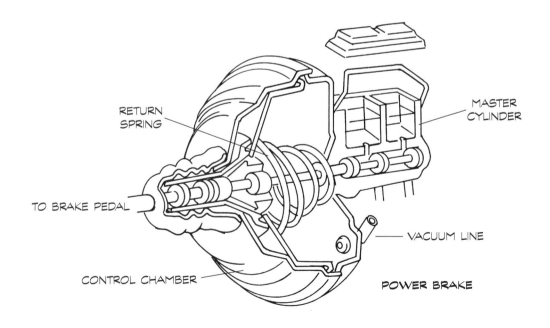

RETURN SPRING

MASTER CYLINDER

TO BRAKE PEDAL

VACUUM LINE

CONTROL CHAMBER

POWER BRAKE

hydraulic assist power brake, common causes of failure are hydraulic pump failure, control valve seizure, or hydraulic leaks. In a hydraulic power brake, the system may also incorporate ANTI-LOCK BRAKE SYSTEM (ABS) pressure controls.

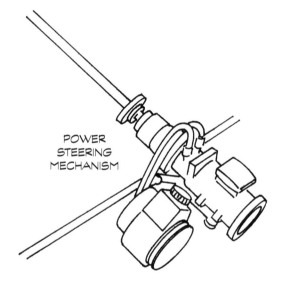 In HYDRAULIC systems, ABS pressures contained are very high, even when the system is off. If so equipped, ABS should be serviced only by a qualified, trained technician.

Powerplant. The powerplant is the source that produces power to move the vehicle. In most modern vehicles, the powerplant is a GASOLINE or DIESEL ENGINE.

Power Steering. Power steering is a steering system using hydraulic pump pressure to assist driver steering force upon the STEERING WHEEL. Most power steering systems today apply HYDRAULIC PRESSURE from an engine-driven hydraulic power steering pump. The power assist pressure is applied to a steering assist piston according to the position of control valves in the STEERING BOX. The control valve regulates the

pressure to the steering box assist piston according to the turning TORQUE that the driver applies to the steering wheel. Problems that occur often stem from low fluid levels that allow air in the system, pump failures, PRESSURE REGULATOR failures, hydraulic leaks, and sticking control valves.

POWER
STEERING
MECHANISM

A power steering system can be checked for pressure assist and control by a qualified technician.

Power Stroke. The power stroke is a PISTON stroke immediately following the COMPRESSION stroke, during which the

VALVEs are closed and the FUEL burns. The stroke lasts from TOP DEAD CENTER (TDC) crank-pin rotation at 0 degrees to BOTTOM DEAD CENTER (BDC) at 180 degrees. During this rotation the expanding compressed gases of fuel burning within the power cycle forces the piston down in the CYLINDER. This transmits power to rotate the CRANKSHAFT through the CONNECTING ROD.

Powertrain. All mechanisms that carry TORQUE from the engine CRANKSHAFT to the vehicle driving WHEELs are called powertrain. Powertrain components include the CLUTCH, FLUID COUPLING or TORQUE CONVERTER, TRANSMISSION, DRIVESHAFT, UNIVERSAL or CONSTANT VELOCITY JOINTS, DIFFERENTIAL, HALFSHAFTS, and AXLES.

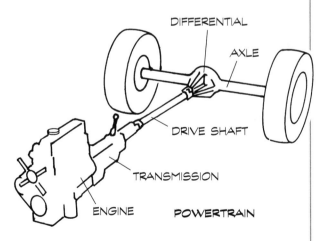

DIFFERENTIAL
AXLE
DRIVE SHAFT
TRANSMISSION
ENGINE   POWERTRAIN

Powertrain Control Module (PCM). The powertrain control module is an electronic computer that receives input from various SENSORs and responds by sending output signals to various POWERTRAIN controls. The PCM, for example, may simultaneously control engine FUEL INJECTION, SPARK PLUG ignitions, and TRANSMISSION gear selections.

Pre-Combustion Chamber. Used in some DIESEL ENGINEs, a pre-combustion chamber is a small, separate COMBUSTION CHAMBER where COMBUSTION begins. The chamber cushions the initial combustion as FUEL INJECTION begins, and allows a turbulent fiery mixture to blow into the main combustion chamber. This usually results in a quieter combustion process that makes pre-combustion chamber diesel engines popular for passenger car use. As well, some pre-combustion chamber engines also incorporate GLOW PLUGS or glow rods. Glow plugs or rods preheat the diesel pre-combustion chamber for easier cold weather starts.

Pre-Ignition. Pre-ignition is the firing of the air/fuel mixture in the engine COM-

BUSTION CHAMBER before the ignition spark occurs at the SPARK PLUG. If pronounced, pre-ignition can cause engine damage. Pressure builds rapidly before or at TOP DEAD CENTER (TDC). The rapid pressure causes the CONNECTING ROD to vibrate. This produces a metal ringing, knocking, or cackling noise. If severe enough, the PISTON crown or piston ring lands may collapse and break.

Causes of pre-ignition include hot spots in a heated engine due to CARBON build-up, an overheated engine, or poor fuel OCTANE RATING.

Preload. Preload is the amount of predetermined load placed on a BEARING before actual operating loads are imposed. The loading prevents shock to bearing rollers when the working load is applied.

Pressure Cap. A pressure cap is located on the RADIATOR inlet. The cap retains the COOLANT, and pressure-activated VALVES within the cap allow fluid to expand and flow either into or out of the coolant overflow tank during engine temperature cycles. The cap maintains system pressures above

atmospheric pressure to prevent coolant from boiling in the ENGINE.

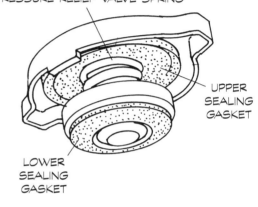

PRESSURE RELIEF VALVE SPRING

UPPER SEALING GASKET

LOWER SEALING GASKET

PRESSURE CAP

Pressure cap holding ability should be checked during regular COOLING SYSTEM services.

Pressure Differential Valve. A pressure differential valve in a split or dual HYDRAULIC BRAKE system illuminates an instrument warning light if the brake pressure drops in one part of the hydraulic system. The warning light informs the driver of a system leak and lowered braking ability.

A vehicle with an illuminated brake warning light should be immediately serviced and repaired.

Pressure Plate. The pressure plate is a spring-loaded metal plate mounted in the CLUTCH housing that rotates with the FLYWHEEL. The pressure plate exerts force against a FRICTION DISC having friction lining similar to BRAKE LINING. At its center, the friction disc splines to the MANUAL TRANSMISSION input shaft.

When the pressure plate springs are applied to the disc by a released CLUTCH PEDAL, the plate holds the clutch friction disc against the flywheel. This action transmits engine TORQUE from the CRANKSHAFT to the TRANSMISSION input shaft.

Pressure Regulator. Used in hydraulic circuits, the pressure regulator is a mechanical metal spool device that vents fluid to control the circuit pressures. In hydraulic systems such as those found in AUTOMATIC TRANSMISSIONs, the regulator valve opens against spring pressure to release fluid when the pressure reaches a specified maximum. This release pressure may be altered (modulated) by an additional spring or HYDRAULIC PRESSUREs. Altering or modulating thus changes the working pressure of the system. By varying pressures in such a way, an auto-matic transmission can offer soft shifts at light throttle settings, and hard, crisp shifts under high engine power demands.

Pressure Relief Valve. A pressure relief valve opens against SPRING tension to relieve excessive pressure. Release tensions on pressure relief valves are not usually modulated. *Also see* PRESSURE REGULATOR.

Pressure Tester. A pressure tester is a diagnostic device that can measure gaseous or liquid pressures. For example, a RADIATOR pressure tester is used to find COOLANT system leaks. Also, a TRANSMISSION pressure tester is used to diagnose AUTOMATIC TRANSMISSION malfunctions. The type of tester used may be specialized for the type of unit being diagnosed.

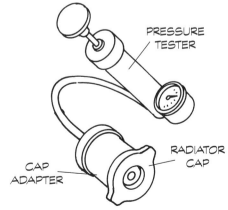

PRESSURE TESTER

CAP ADAPTER

RADIATOR CAP

Pressurize. To apply mechanical force to a GAS or liquid to acquire more than atmospheric pressure.

Preventive Maintenance. Service done to a vehicle according to a preset schedule is called preventive maintenance. Examples are engine OIL changes, FILTER replacements, DRIVE BELT adjustments or inspections, CHASSIS lubrications, WHEEL BEARING repack, etc. Preventive maintenance listings may be found in a vehicle owner manual. It is recommended that these time or mileage intervals be met or preempted for maximum vehicle service life.

Primary Circuit. The BATTERY or low-voltage CIRCUIT of an IGNITION SYSTEM is called the primary circuit, including the primary winding of the COIL(s).

PROM (Programmable Read Only Memory). A PROM is a replaceable computer chip that designates all of the calibration settings. PROMs are programmed for a specific POWERTRAIN.

 PROM updates are sometimes available for specific driveability complaints. See your vehicle manufacturer or service technician.

Propeller Shaft. The propeller shaft is a longitudinal shaft used to transmit TORQUE. The propeller shaft is also called the DRIVESHAFT.

Proportioning Valve. A proportioning valve is a hydraulic control VALVE that reduces BRAKE application pressure to the vehicle rear WHEELs during hard braking. This action compensates for vehicle weight shift that occurs during hard braking and helps to prevent rear wheel skid.

Pull. Vehicle drift or steering toward one side during normal driving on a level surface is called pull. Pull can occur when the vehicle is moving with the BRAKES released. Therefore pull may be caused by WHEEL ALIGNMENT error, uneven TIRE pressures, tire mismatch, or brake dragging. Pull can also occur when the brakes are applied.

 Pull while braking is usually caused by an imbalance of HYDRAULIC PRESSURE to the wheels, or uneven BRAKE LINING friction ability.

Purge Canister. *See* CHARCOAL CANISTER.

Purge Valve. A purge valve is used in evaporative EMISSION CONTROL systems. The purge valve is used in the CHARCOAL CANISTER venting. The charcoal canister, connected by vapor lines to the FUEL TANK, stores evaporative GASOLINE fumes from the tank. When the ENGINE starts, the valve allows purging of the stored fumes to the intake system of the engine. The engine consumes the fumes during warm-up and normal operation, therefore limiting the escape of FUEL vapors to the atmosphere.

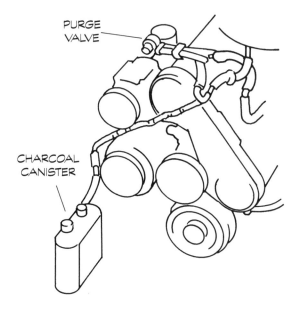

Pushrod. The pushrod is a VALVETRAIN component that transmits cam FOLLOWER or LIFTER motion to the valve operating ROCKER ARM. Pushrods may be solid rods, or hollow tubes. If hollow, they often are used to route lubricating oil to the ROCKER ARM and valve stems. Pushrods, especially the hollow variety, are subject to bending due to excessively high ENGINE revolutions, sticking VALVES, or excess VALVE SPRING tensions.

PVS. *See* PORTED VACUUM SWITCH.

❋

Quad Carburetor. A quad carburetor has four airflow PORTs and THROTTLE PLATEs for the control of the engine's air/fuel mixture. Normally two ports are used to deliver air/fuel mixture during idle and light throttle position cruising. The secondary throttle ports open and provide a greater volume of air/fuel mixture during high engine power output operations, such as when PASSING GEAR is used.

Quadrant Gear. A quadrant gear is a toothed GEAR that is arc-shaped in a quarter circle. A quadrant gear is used in some window glass REGULATORs to provide mechanical arm motion for raising and lowering the window glass. Quadrant gear use is usually coupled with manual operation or a reversible DC electric MOTOR.

Quadrant Shift Indicator. A quadrant shift indicator is a quarter circle INSTRUMENT PANEL indicator that shows the operator which AUTOMATIC TRANSMISSION operation range is selected.

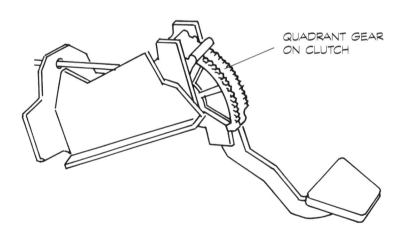

QUADRANT GEAR
ON CLUTCH

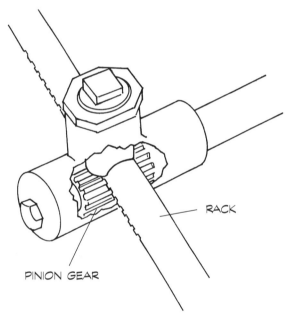

RACK-AND-PINION STEERING

Races. Races are hardened metal surfaces or rings on which ball or roller BEARINGs rotate. Races can fail due to lack of lubrication, dirt and foreign object contamination, inadequate tension, insufficient running CLEARANCEs, and excess load, speed, or heat.

Rack-and-Pinion Steering. A rack-and-pinion steering system has a gear box containing a longitudinal gear rack and a PINION GEAR that moves the rack in lateral directions. The pinion gear connects to the steering wheel shaft. As the STEERING WHEEL is turned by the driver, the pinion rotates. The pinion meshes with gear teeth on the rack. The turning action pushes or pulls the rack laterally to steer the vehicle to the left or right.

The rack ends are equipped with BALLJOINTs that move the STEERING ARMs of the wheel spindles or KNUCKLEs. For the modern automobile, this design has the advantage of lightweight and slim design. And, like the RECIRCULATING BALL STEERING unit, rack-and-pinion steering is offered with hydraulic power-assisted steering.

Radial Tire. A radial tire is constructed by the manufacturer so that the PLIES of supporting materials are placed radially, or perpendicular to the TIRE body and WHEEL rim. The radial tire body has a circumferential belt that surrounds the radial PLIES. During manufacture, the circumferential belt receives an overlay of tire TREAD. Radial tire design advantages include good tread contact with the highway surface, especially during vehicle turns.

Radiator. A radiator is used in the engine cooling system. The radiator is a heat exchanger that contains COOLANT fluid. A radiator cools the fluid passing through it via heat transfer to the air flowing past the radiator cooling tubes and fins. The radiator receives hot fluid from the ENGINE, cools the fluid, and returns it to the engine.

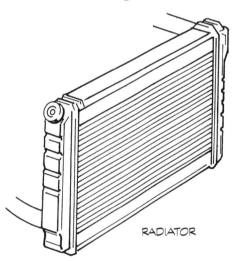

RADIATOR

 Radiator cooling function can be impeded by clogged or damaged

grille area, foreign objects accumulated on the cooling fins, and internal clogging of the tubes. Some cooling system malfunctions may appear as radiator overheating, with an underlying root cause such as a stuck engine THERMO-STAT, a defective cooling FAN operation, or WATER PUMP failure. Radiators are tested for their pressure holding ability, heat dissipation, and flow rate.

 Never open a hot or over-heating radiator.

Radius Arm. *See* LONGITUDINAL ARM, LEADING ARM, *and* TRAILING ARM.

Rag Joint. A rag joint is a flexible fiber cloth joint used to couple the steering column center shaft to the steering box INPUT SHAFT. The joint allows the STEERING WHEEL rotation to transmit to the STEERING BOX through minor angle changes without pulsation. It also allows slight changes to occur in STEERING SHAFT length and position due to vehicle body and CHASSIS flex. The joint also dampens the transmission of road noises to the STEERING COLUMN.

 If defective, the rag joint can cause steering wheel play. The joint usually contains fail-safe pins that will allow steering, though very loose, if the joint completely fails.

Rear-Wheel Drive. A system of engine power flow that delivers the motive TORQUE to the vehicle's rear WHEELs through a TRANSMISSION and DIFFERENTIAL.

Receiver. Used in automotive air conditioning refrigeration circuits, the receiver or RECEIVER-DRIER receives liquid REFRIGERANT from the CONDENSER. In older vehicles, the unit may sport a SIGHT GLASS so that any bubbles in the refrigerant may be seen by a technician.

Receiver-Drier. *See* RECEIVER.

Recirculating Ball Steering. A recirculating ball steering unit uses recirculating balls that roll on a worm gear. The GEAR and balls move a ball-driven nut and the pinion shaft. STEERING WHEEL motion caused by the driver rotates the worm gear. The motion transfers through the recirculating balls to the ball nut. The ball nut, in turn, meshes with a SECTOR GEAR and the pinion shaft. The pinion shaft

swings the PITMAN ARM and moves the STEERING LINKAGE.

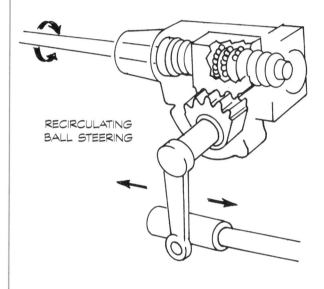

RECIRCULATING
BALL STEERING

Recirculating ball steering can be manual or power-assisted. The steering unit can be affected by worn parts or lack of adjustment. Internal looseness or insecure STEERING BOX mounting can cause vehicle steering wander. Metal fatigue and lubrication loss can cause binding.

Also, POWER STEERING pump failure can cause loss of steering assist. Steering assist differences during left to right turning may suffer from failures in the unit's left/right hydraulic steering control VALVE.

Rectifier. A rectifier is a DIODE, usually used in the ALTERNATOR, that changes alternator output from ALTERNATING CURRENT (AC) to DIRECT CURRENT (DC).

Failure of the unit causes alternator output to allow BATTERY depletion. A defective rectifier can be detected by alternator output waveform testing.

Refrigerant. Refrigerant is a substance having a low evaporation temperature that transfers heat in an AIR CONDITIONING SYSTEM. Heat transfers to the refrigerant in the EVAPORATOR, thus cooling the air flowing past the evaporator tubes and fins. The heat then dissipates in the CONDENSER, transferring to air flowing through the condenser unit.

Two refrigerants are in use in today's automobiles, R-12 and R-134a. R-12 is an older refrigerant-type used in prior year auto manufacturing. R-12 was found to be chemically harmful to the environment, and is now superseded by R-134a. If an older vehicle requires repair and replacement of the refrigerant, an R-12 substitution procedure must occur. The system must be modified to operate with the later chemistry refrigerant.

For major repairs to an air conditioning system to occur, the refrigerant is removed and the system is vacuumed of air and moisture content before recharging. This must occur to keep moisture-laden air from the CIRCUIT. Moisture will freeze control VALVES and the system can malfunction.

Do not disconnect and open the refrigerant circuit of an automobile. Refrigerant that vents to the atmosphere can cause injury to exposed skin. The handling of refrigerant under pressure in an air conditioning system requires training and proper safety equipment. Environmental regulations dictate that the recharge and replacement of the air conditioning refrigerant should only be accomplished by qualified technicians government-certified in proper refrigerant handling procedures and precautions.

Regulator. A regulator is a device that exercises control. In the BATTERY charging system, for example, the VOLTAGE REGULATOR is a device that controls ALTERNATOR voltage output. In a power window, the window regulator controls the up and down motion of the window glass.

Relay. An electrical device that operates a SECONDARY CIRCUIT continuity in response to a primary voltage signal is called a relay. For example, a STARTER MOTOR relay uses a low amperage signal provided through the IGNITION SWITCH to control the high amperage current to the starter motor. The use of the relay thus saves the ignition switch from the burning effects of high current flow.

Release Bearing. Also called the THROWOUT BEARING. The release bearing is used in a mechanical CLUTCH to move the clutch PRESSURE PLATE. The release bearing rides on an arm worked by LINKAGE or cable from the driver's CLUTCH PEDAL. The arm moves the release bearing in or out of contact with the clutch fingers. In doing so, the release bearing operates the clutch levers of the spinning clutch. As the levers move, the clutch pressure plate moves. The clutch thus clamps or releases the CLUTCH DISC. The clutch disc connects by SPLINEs at its center to the transmission INPUT SHAFT.

A clutch can slip because of inadequate BEARING motion. This occurs as the clutch fingers do not fully release from the bearing. The full force of the clutch SPRINGs are not allowed to clamp the clutch disc, and the bearing keeps spinning and prematurely wears.

Also, the clutch disc can drag because the arm motion does not fully depress the bearing to release the clutch pressure plate. Dragging may cause difficulty shifting, and clashing or grinding of transmission GEARs and SYNCHRONIZERS.

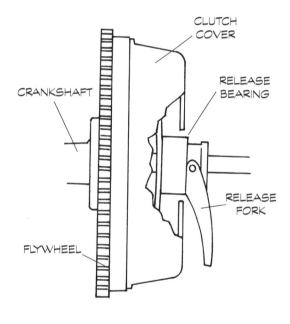

The clutch release bearing CLEARANCE should be adjusted according to manufacturer schedules or before. The clutch release bearing is normally replaced during clutch service.

Relief Valve. A relief valve opens when a preset liquid or vapor pressure is reached, to relieve pressure and prevent damage or physical harm. For example, if equipped, a high pressure relief valve may protect an air conditioning COMPRESSOR against the destructive effects of excess REFRIGERANT pressure.

Reluctor. A reluctor is a metal ROTOR or ARMATURE in an electronic system that detects the rotational position of a component by sensing a metal bump, protrusion, or GAP. The reluctor creates a voltage signal in the electromagnetic PICKUP COIL as each metal portion of the reluctor passes by. Among other applications, a reluctor may be used in an IGNITION SYSTEM as an engine position SENSOR. Also a reluctor may detect wheel speed for an ANTI-LOCK BRAKE SYSTEM computer.

Reserve Capacity. Referring to a BATTERY, reserve capacity is the number of minutes the battery can support a 25 AMPERE current load before the cell voltages fall to 1.75 volts for each cell. *Also see* COLD CRANKING RATE.

Resistance. Used as an electrical term, resistance to current flow (amperage) is measured by the ohm scale. *Also see* VOLT, AMPERE, *and* OHM.

Resonator. A resonator is used in some engine EXHAUST SYSTEMS as an additional noise muffling device. Usually used in conjunction with a muffler, the unit is located toward the end of the exhaust TAILPIPE. *See* MUFFLER.

Retard. Retard is understood by the automotive technician as the delay of a SPARK PLUG firing in the COMBUSTION CHAMBER. Generally, an excessive spark retard causes power cycle pressures to fall, resulting in sluggish ENGINE performance and high EXHAUST EMISSIONS.

Return. Return is the tendency of front wheels to return to the straight-ahead position when the driver releases tension on the STEERING WHEEL after turning. Return tendency is greatly affected by the front wheel CASTER settings. A failure to return may indicate WHEEL ALIGNMENT error, binding steering, or improper power-assist operation.

Return Spring. A return spring is a spring that restores a component to a rest position. For example, a BRAKE return spring returns an applied brake SHOE and BRAKE LINING to its rest position.

Rheostat. A rheostat is a variable resistor that changes voltage or current through an electric CIRCUIT. For example, on some vehicles a driver turns the HEADLIGHT switch knob to change the brightness of the INSTRUMENT PANEL lighting. The SWITCH usually contains a rheostat that alters the voltage available to the light circuit.

Ring Gear. A ring gear is a large GEAR on the DIFFERENTIAL final drive. The ring gear is carried by the differential housing or case. The ring gear meshes with the final drive pinion, also known as the PINION GEAR. The TORQUE delivered to the ring gear by the pinion, rotates the ring gear and the differential housing and gears. The differential, in turn, drives the AXLE SHAFTs.

The ring gear rotation thus causes the WHEELs to rotate and the vehicle to move. A ring gear is precision matched to fit its drive pinion gear. Both GEARs receive special high strength and wear characteristics through hardening.

If differential whine, growl, or rumbling occurs as a result of gear-set failure, the gears and supporting bearings should be replaced.

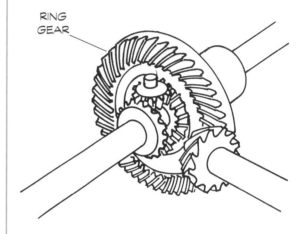

RING GEAR

RING GEAR IN A DIFFERENTIAL

Ring Ridge. Ring ridge is a metal ridge outcropping that forms at the top of a CYLINDER wall as the PISTON and its rings wear into the ENGINE BLOCK. Created above the highest wear point in the cylinder by COMBUSTION, the RING RIDGE must be removed before the piston and PISTON RINGS are extracted for repairs or replacement. Technicians use a special tool called a ridge reamer to accomplish the task without damaging nearby cylinder wall areas.

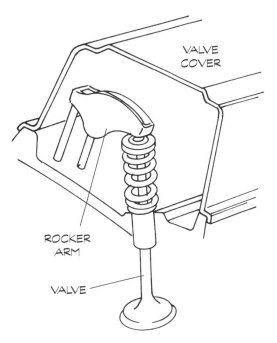

Rocker Arm. A rocker arm is a lever that pivots to transfer CAM or PUSHROD motion to an INTAKE VALVE or EXHAUST VALVE. A rocker arm may be adjustable to offer valve CLEARANCEs or centering of FOLLOWER hydraulic pistons. Adjustment, if possible, is done with both CAM LOBEs positioned on the base circle, offering no lift to the valve. The adjustment procedure must be accomplished by a technician familiar with the ENGINE VALVE opening order, or major damage could occur.

If the adjustment is not made in the correct sequence, bent valves, bent VALVETRAIN parts, or PISTON damage may result.

Roller Lifter. *See* ROLLER TAPPET.

Roller Tappet. Also termed ROLLER LIFTER, the roller tappet is a VALVE LIFTER that contains an AXLE that carries a hardened steel roller. The roller rides against the camshaft lobe to open the ENGINE VALVE(s) against VALVE SPRING force. The unit provides valve action with very low FRICTION loss and CAMSHAFT wear.

Rotary Engine. The rotary engine is a gas WANKEL engine, in which the power is delivered from a spinning ROTOR(s). While rotary engines have been tested

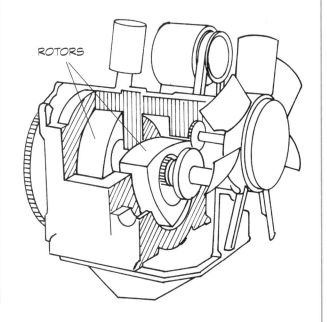

and offered in passenger car applications, widespread use has not been a result.

Rotation. The swapping of WHEEL position to provide maximum tire life. Wheels are swapped from front to rear or in an "x" pattern.

See your vehicle manufacturer or service technician for inspection and service intervals. Also called TIRE ROTATION.

Rotor. The rotating portion or part of a machine is often called the rotor. Examples of rotors are found in an ALTERNATOR, a DISC BRAKE, an IGNITION DISTRIBUTOR, or a ROTARY ENGINE.

Run On. *See* DIESELING.

Runout. An out-of-round or wobble condition in a rotating part is called runout. For example, WHEEL runout may cause vibration or steering wobble.

Excess runout may cause erroneous alignment if a bent wheel is used during a WHEEL ALIGNMENT.

Runout may also exist in a BRAKE DISC or BRAKE DRUM. The condition may cause a vibration of the BRAKE PEDAL beneath a driver's foot as the BRAKE is applied. At times runout is most pronounced under light braking. Runout is causing the HYDRAULIC BRAKE piston to return HYDRAULIC pulsations to the MASTER CYLINDER, and therefore to the brake pedal.

In wheel runout, replacing of the offending wheel rim, and possibly the TIRE, usually cures the problem. Also, if left unrepaired, the runout condition may cause high wear to steering and SUSPENSION parts.

Brake runout causes high wear of brake components and instability in braking action. The machining of a brake drum or brake disc may repair the condition. Occasionally, the drum or disc must be replaced to correct a runout condition.

Schrader Valve. A Schrader valve allows air or gauge connection to a TIRE or air conditioning REFRIGERANT system.

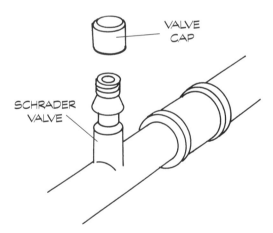 The Schrader valve must be kept free of dirt and moisture contamination. This indicates that whenever pressure is tested or services are required, the service cap should be immediately reinstalled afterward.

VALVE CAP

SCHRADER VALVE

Scrub Radius. Scrub radius is also termed as the STEERING OFFSET. The scrub radius is the measured distance difference between the STEERING KNUCK-

LE vertical PIVOT axis centerline and the TIRE centerline where these intersect the road surface.

A check of scrub radius should be an integral part of a WHEEL ALIGNMENT. Error in scrub radius shown between left and right side front wheels during wheel alignment may indicate bent steering system parts. Additional diagnosis and part measurements usually reveals the defect or damage.

Seal. A seal is a material, usually rubber, rope, or cork composition, that is shaped around a shaft to prevent liquid, gaseous, or GREASE leakage. For example, a seal at both ends of a shaft enclose the lubricant to prevent loss and protect the enclosed area from dirt and debris.

Secondary Circuit. The secondary circuit relates to the IGNITION SYSTEM portion that delivers high spark plug voltage. Secondary circuit components may include the COIL or several coils, high voltage (tension) wires, high tension DISTRIBUTOR devices such as the ROTOR and DISTRIBUTOR CAP, and each SPARK PLUG.

Sector Gear. A sector gear is a section of a circular GEAR that does not form a complete circle. For example, a sector gear may be used in a window REGULATOR. The sector gear provides the needed up or down arm motion of the lever that raises and lowers the window.

Segment. The sections or bars of an electrical COMMUTATOR are termed segments. Segments are found on the ARMATURE of a STARTER MOTOR or GENERATOR. If a segment, normally insulated from another, contacts an adjacent segment because of heat damage or BEARING wear, the unit shorts and loses proper current flow characteristics. With a starter motor, the result is a very high BATTERY current draw when the ENGINE is cranked for starting, and the cranking speed is usually slowed.

Self-Adjuster. A self-adjuster is a mechanism that makes up for mechanical wear or needed repositioning. For example, a self-adjuster is normally found in DRUM BRAKES. The adjuster compensates for BRAKE LINING wear by adjusting the brake shoe running CLEARANCE. In many vehicles, the adjustment takes place when the vehicle is operated in reverse and the brakes are applied.

A self-adjuster, however, can malfunction and cause brake pulling, brake overheating, and premature lining wear. Lack of adjustment and low BRAKE PEDAL can also occur.

Each time a brake lining is replaced, the brake adjuster needs to be serviced and checked for proper function.

Self-Diagnostic. A self-diagnostic system shows a warning to the vehicle operator or repair technician when a malfunction occurs. As trouble occurs, the system senses electrical information and may turn on a MALFUNCTION INDICATOR LIGHT (MIL). When quizzed by a technician using appropriate test equipment or ON-BOARD DIAGNOSTIC (OBD) procedures, the system usually displays a DIAGNOSTIC TROUBLE CODE or codes indicating the fault. Modern vehicles have a system that has standardized the coded messages given by the computer. The codes, called OBD codes, are translated into a suggested diagnostic path area that will require additional testing for problem diagnosis and correction.

Sensor. A sensor is a device that reacts to changing electrical voltages, current flow, temperature, pressure, light, mechanical position, etc. The sensor sends the necessary measured information to a RELAY, CONTROLLER, or computer.

Sequential Fuel Injection. A Sequential Fuel Injection (SFI) is a system of FUEL INJECTION where the firing of the injection nozzles agree with the firing order or INTAKE VALVE operating sequences. *Also see* PORT FUEL INJECTION.

Series Circuit. A series circuit is an electric CIRCUIT that connects electrical devices in sequential series. The connections route POSITIVE terminal to NEGATIVE terminal then again positive to negative, repeating as necessary through all terminals. The same cur-

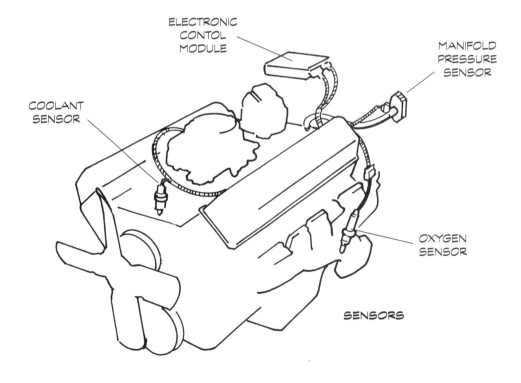

SENSORS

rent flows through all the devices in the circuit. Voltage (electrical push) diminishes, stepping down as ELECTRONs push through each RESISTANCE.

Servo. A servo is an electrical, pneumatic, or HYDRAULIC device that produces motion. In electrical application, a servo may produce a linear or rotary arc in response to changing voltage or current flow. In pneumatic or hydraulic systems, a servo is a PISTON usually having a spring-resistance included, that converts applied pressure to mechanical movement. A servo may apply a transmission band, or be placed in a hydraulic BAND or CLUTCH apply circuit to tailor or cushion the shift feel of the unit. Usually hydraulic servos have metal rings or rubber SEALs that guard against hydraulic leaks.

The replacement of servo rings or seals is part of TRANSMISSION repair or rebuilding procedures.

Setback. Setback is a measured difference in vehicle front to rear WHEELBASE from side to side. If incorrect, the setback measurement can detect WHEEL ALIGNMENT error, body or FRAME misalignment, or a bent SUSPENSION part.

Shackle. A shackle is a support for one end of a LEAF spring. Attaching the SPRING to the vehicle body or FRAME, the shackle allows the flex of the leaf spring to lengthen or shorten according to its flexing action. Shackles are made of hardened steel for strength and should not be replaced with mild or soft steel substitutes.

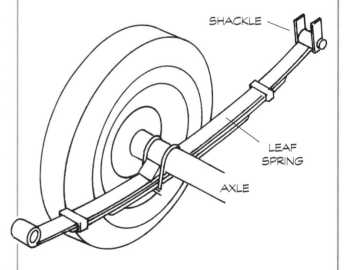

Also, changes to the shackle should not be accomplished to correct vehicle ride height troubles. Always replace (rather than repair) a damaged SPRING or springs.

Shift Solenoid. A shift solenoid is a computer-controlled SOLENOID, used in an electronic-controlled AUTOMATIC TRANSMISSION that controls hydraulic fluid passage. The electrical signal activates the solenoid magnet to influence the position of a cylindrical or poppet VALVE. The valve thereby controls the application pressures to various BANDS, CLUTCHes, or TRANSMISSION circuits.

Shift Valve. A shift valve is a hydraulic control VALVE that moves to produce a HYDRAULIC PRESSURE routing change in an AUTOMATIC TRANSMISSION. The routing change applies or removes hydraulic pressures to the hydraulic CLUTCH apply PISTONs or band SERVOs. A shift valve operation may be altered by SOLE-NOIDS, VACUUM MODULATOR action, THROT-TLE position, road speed sensing, and other TIMING devices.

A TRANSMISSION's inability to shift or sequence properly through its gear ranges should be investigated by a trained automatic transmission repair technician.

Shock Absorber. A shock absorber is a hydraulic PISTON device, usually tubu-

lar in design, that is attached to the CHASSIS at each vehicle WHEEL. The shock absorber regulates and quickly diminishes LEAF spring flex, or COIL spring compression and rebound. Shock absorbers are available from car makers and aftermarket sources in a wide variety of standard and heavy-duty versions, with varying road and ride adjusting qualities.

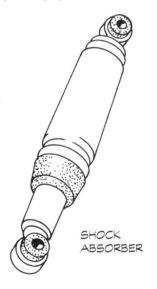

SHOCK ABSORBER

Choose replacements according to the type of driving encountered and the recommendations of a qualified service technician.

Shoe. Shoe is a term used to describe a rubbing segment of material. In an elec-

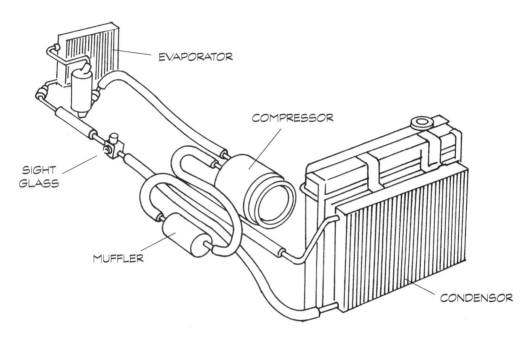

EVAPORATOR

COMPRESSOR

SIGHT GLASS

MUFFLER

CONDENSOR

tric MOTOR, GENERATOR, or ALTERNATOR, the term shoe may indicate the BRUSH that delivers electricity to or from an ARMATURE. In the BRAKE system, the shoe is an arc-shaped metal plate that supports the BRAKE LINING. The shoe absorbs shock and heat as it transmits braking force to the brake mounting or backing plate. The brake lining attaches to the metal shoe using rivets or bonding cement.

Short Circuit. A short circuit is a current path that allows electrical flow to circumvent the CIRCUIT load. The short usually lightens the circuit RESISTANCE and increases current flow to the point that fuses blow, CIRCUIT BREAKERs pop, or wires burn. A short may be occa-sional, requiring certain conditions be met. For example, a short circuit may occur in a STOP LIGHT circuit only after a period of rain. Moisture leaking from road spray gets into the stop light housing, offering a short circuit. The low resistance blows the FUSE when the BRAKE is applied.

Noting the conditions occurring at the time of the function loss, therefore, is an important part of short diagnosis. Shorts can be investigated by a technician using a short finder and multimeter.

Sight Glass. A sight glass is a small viewing window in the REFRIGERANT circuit of an automotive's AIR CONDITIONING

SYSTEM. The glass offers a view of refrigerant as it passes through the CIRCUIT toward the EVAPORATOR. Excess bubbling of the refrigerant can indicate air in the circuit, and other indications can signal various troubles in the system. The sight glass has been omitted from the refrigeration circuits of many modern vehicles.

Silicone Rubber. Silicone rubber is a material similar to aerobic GASKET material used to seal specific type of automotive parts when joined. Silicone rubber is especially fitted for mating components having COOLANT circulation. In general, because of its specific rubbery qualities, silicone rubber gasketing is not generally used in AUTOMATIC TRANSMISSION repairs. The rubber-like consistency does not blend well with TRANSMISSION functions if the gasketing material enters the fluid stream.

Note: Silicone Rubber should not be used on vehicles equipped with oxygen sensors. Sensor failure will occur.

Single-Point Injection (SBI). *See* THROTTLE BODY FUEL INJECTION.

Slip Joint. A slip joint, sometimes called the SLIP YOKE, is a splined mechanical connection in the DRIVETRAIN. Usually in the DRIVESHAFT, the slip joint allows changes in length. For example, the use of a slip joint in the driveshaft or a REAR-WHEEL DRIVE (RWD) vehicle allows the AXLE housing (sometimes called the THIRD MEMBER) to travel vertically and adjust for changes in vehicle carrying height. The vertical housing movement causes a slight change necessary in driveshaft length, provided by the slip joint. Also, during BRAKE applications, the rear housing reacts to the TIRE traction, this causes a needed driveshaft lengthening. The slip joint or SLIP YOKE later retracts as the vehicle weight transfers to normal riding height. Sometimes, if slip joint or slip yoke lubrication is deficient, a popping, burping or groaning noise is heard as the vehicle stops and/or the brake is released.

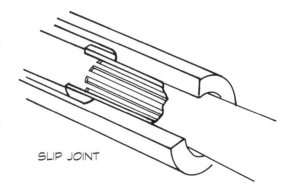

SLIP JOINT

Slip Ring. A slip ring is found in the ALTERNATOR or sometimes in an A/C COMPRESSOR CLUTCH. A slip ring forms the rotating connections between the spinning windings and the stationary brushes. Usually made of copper or copper alloy, the slip rings must remain smooth and clean to allow good contact for the electrical flow from the winding. Burns or pitting of the surfaces destroys the electrical transmitting abilities of the rings.

Slip Yoke. *See* SLIP JOINT.

Solar Cell. A solar cell is an electrical unit that generates a small DC voltage when exposed to light. A solar cell may be used in a modern vehicle to maintain a BATTERY charge during prolonged vehicle storage.

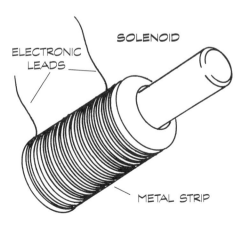

Solenoid. A solenoid is an electrical device that produces a mechanical push/pull movement when connected to a power source. The solenoid usually contains an ELECTROMAGNET that operates an action rod when current flows through the solenoid CIRCUIT.

Solid State. Solid state is an electrical device, such as a TRANSISTOR, that contains no moving mechanical parts. The component relies upon the movement of ELECTRONs for the performance of tasks.

South Pole. The south pole of a magnet, opposite the NORTH POLE, is the pole at which the magnetic lines of force reenter a magnet. In MAGNETIC FORCE, the south pole pushes another south pole away, or attracts a north pole.

Spark Advance. *See* ADVANCE.

Spark Ignition Engine. An ENGINE operating on FUEL that is ignited by the heat from an electric SPARK PLUG is a spark ignition engine. Examples are the GASOLINE engine and natural gas engine.

Spark Plug. The spark plug provides an

ELECTRONIC LEADS

SOLENOID

METAL STRIP

electrical spark in the ENGINE cylinder at the end of the COMPRESSION cycle, to fire the cylinder air/fuel mixture. The spark plug contains a pair of electrodes and an electrical insulator. The center metal ELECTRODE runs through the spark plug insulator body and into the tip. It carries the high-voltage electric charge to the spark plug air gap. The insulator body prevents grounding of the voltage potential and is made of porcelain material. At the spark plug tip, the high-voltage charge builds and jumps across the air GAP to the ground electrode. The heat generated during the spark jump fires the combustible air/fuel mixture in the CYLINDER.

Available in various electrode configurations, spark plugs are rated according to heat range and tip reach into the

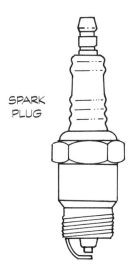

SPARK
PLUG

cylinder. Spark plugs are normally considered as consumables. Therefore, spark plugs wear due to electrical deterioration and deposition and are replaced at recommended times or mileage intervals.

The replacement interval normally observed is called the TUNE-UP period. As the tune-up becomes due, the spark plugs and other items governing engine efficiency are replaced or maintained.

Specific Gravity. Specific gravity is a measurement of an automotive wet-cell BATTERY charge. Specific gravity is the weight-per-unit volume of a substance as compared with the weight-per-unit volume of water. The battery cell's acid content comparison to the water content indicates the cell charge.

A battery that is properly charged for a recommended time period, and fails a specific gravity test afterward, is recommended for replacement as having a defective cell.

Speedometer. The speedometer is the display in the driver's INSTRUMENT PANEL that shows the speed of vehicle travel. Speedometers may be calibrated in U.S. standard miles or metric kilometers per hour, or both. The speedometer may be operated mechanically by a drive CABLE connected to the TRANSMISSION output or a WHEEL of the vehicle. The unit may also be ELECTRONIC in design and operate from a transmission output shaft SENSOR or driveshaft sensor. Speedometers normally also carry the ODOMETER and possibly a trip odometer. The odometer provides a reading on the total forward distance driven by the vehicle. Odometer tampering is illegal in most instances, unless the speedometer is replaced. Whenever odometer replacement is necessary, note is made of the mileage inaccuracy for the benefit of future vehicle owners. The trip odometer usually has a button that is pushed for resetting the dial to zero. Once set, the trip odometer displays the distance traveled from the last setting.

Speedometer repairs are not usually done by a service technician, but replacements may be done at the automobile dealer or their recommended agency.

Spline. A spline is a joint that mates two rotating shaft sections together. A driveline SLIP JOINT allows changes to occur in overall shaft length. The spline contains internal and external mating teeth, similar to GEAR teeth. The teeth slide together and apart in their mating length according to the shaft's length change needs. Splines require adequate, and often special, lubrication.

Used predominately in a vehicle's DRIVESHAFT or in independent AXLE SHAFTs, a spline should receive inspection and lubrication during vehicle services.

Spool Valve. A spool valve is a cylindrical VALVE used to control OIL flow in hydraulic systems such as the circuits of an AUTOMATIC TRANSMISSION, POWER STEERING, ABS HYDRAULIC BRAKE BOOSTER, or other HYDRAULIC components. The spool valve contains outer circumference lands that seal against the bore wall of a drilled and honed passage. The valve has valley areas between the lands that carry pressurized liquid to bore PORTs. The ports thereby deliver pressurized fluid to the intended destination. Spool valves are often housed in a unit called the VALVE BODY.

Sprag Clutch. A sprag clutch is a one-way or single-direction rotation mechanical device often found in AUTOMATIC TRANSMISSIONS or OVERDRIVE units. Looking somewhat like a BEARING, the sprag clutch (or ONE WAY CLUTCH) contains eccentric or S-shaped locking rollers or elements that can lock and transmit TORQUE in one direction, but not in the other. During the torque reversal reaction, the sprag clutch freewheels with little drag. If a sprag clutch fails, the TRANSMISSION or unit loses all drive in that operational GEAR range. Metal particles subsequently pollute the oiling or lubrication system of the unit.

In an automatic transmission, a total rebuild and cleaning of the transmission is often recommended if a sprag clutch fails. The sprag clutch also finds use in the TORQUE CONVERTER.

Spring. A spring is a LEAF or COIL device that changes shape under stress or force. The spring, usually a tempered device, returns to the original shape when the distorting stress or force

abates. In an automobile SUSPENSION system, the spring absorbs rapid road surface level changes by flexing.

SPRING

Sprung. The weight of a vehicle that is supported by the SUSPENSION springs.

Stabilizer Bar. Often called a SWAY BAR, the stabilizer bar is a high-tension steel bar connected transversely across the SUSPENSION. The bar reduces auto body roll on turns and sway on rough, uneven surfaces. Stabilizer bars are calibrated to the vehicle weight by strength and thickness. Though a stabilizer bar seldom breaks, they can become weakened and cause uneven vehicle ride height. Stabilizer bars also have supporting rubber BUSHINGs and grommets that can deteriorate.

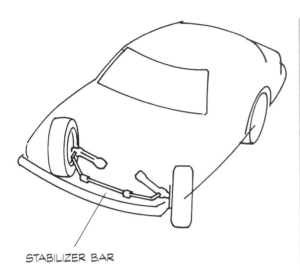

STABILIZER BAR

If rubber parts fail, the vehicle driver may note a metal clanking or rattling on bumpy roads, made quiet by vehicle turns and body tilt. If stabilizer bar rubber BUSHINGs or grommets fail, they should be immediately replaced.

Starter. *See* STARTER MOTOR.

Starter Bendix Drive. *See* STARTER MOTOR DRIVE.

Starter Motor. A starter motor, often simply termed as the starter, is a powerful electric MOTOR that converts electrical current and the resulting MAGNETISM into mechanical energy sufficient enough to spin the engine CRANKSHAFT.

If the starter ARMATURE fails, the unit usually won't operate due to an open CIRCUIT, or it may growl due to an electrical short. Starter BUSHINGs also may fail, causing the starter motor armature to rub against the magnetic fields and wear through insulation. A burned or pitted current control SOLENOID may also prevent a good starter motor electric current path. This causes the circuit or starter motor to malfunction when the ignition key is placed in the "start" position.

The starter solenoid may also stick in the closed-circuit position, causing the starter motor to continue to drive after the ENGINE starts. This action usually causes starter motor and FLYWHEEL, FLEX PLATE, or torque converter RING GEAR damage due to BENDIX unit overspeed.

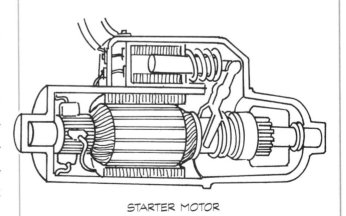

STARTER MOTOR

Starters may be tested using a heavy-duty electrical meter and engine r.p.m. gauge. Replacement of some starter units may require a change of mounting shims. The shims locate the starter drive gear properly to the engine flywheel, flex plate, or TORQUE CONVERTER drive gear teeth.

Starter Motor Drive. Sometimes called the STARTER BENDIX DRIVE, the starter motor drive GEAR rides on the end of the starter motor ARMATURE shaft. As the STARTER MOTOR spins, the gear engages with the FLYWHEEL or TORQUE CONVERTER ring-gear teeth. The starter motor can therefore spin the ENGINE to start it. Depending on starter design, the drive can be inertial or positive. An inertial Bendix indicates that the drive inserts to the flywheel teeth via TORQUE reaction. Once engaged the drive rotates the engine. After the engine starts, the drive disengages using one-way CLUTCH and SPRING action as the increased engine flywheel speed and release of the ignition key ceases the Bendix unit application torque.

A positive starter motor drive uses a mounted SOLENOID and drive YOKE action on the starter motor. The yoke mechanically inserts the drive gear into the flywheel gear teeth just before the starter motor solenoid allows the starter motor to spin. After an engine start, the drive gear's one-way SPRAG CLUTCH prevents overspeed damage until the starter motor operation ceases and the solenoid return spring backs the drive gear out of the flywheel gear teeth.

The starter motor drive can lose its engine rotating ability due to failures of the starter motor, solenoid, Bendix, or yoke. Starter noise can also sound out loudly after the engine starts if the Bendix return spring breaks or the yoke fails to disengage the Bendix gear. The starter can also clash noisily if the GEAR does not mate properly with the flywheel teeth or disengage in a timely fashion. Damage to the flywheel teeth often means flywheel, FLEX PLATE, or torque converter replacement.

Static Balance. Static balance is the balance of a rotating object while it is not moving. Errors in balance may be corrected by the adding or removing of circumferential weight.

Stator. The stator is a stationary mem-

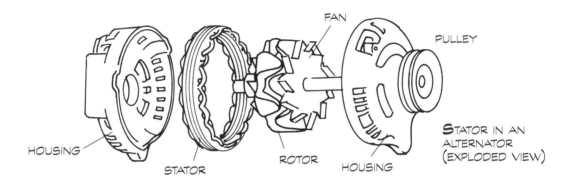

FAN

PULLEY

HOUSING

STATOR

ROTOR

HOUSING

STATOR IN AN ALTERNATOR (EXPLODED VIEW)

ber of an electric MOTOR or GENERATOR, in which a ROTOR revolves. In the ALTERNATOR, for example, the stator contains the conductors and induces electricity into the rotor.

In an AUTOMATIC TRANSMISSION, the TORQUE CONVERTER contains a stator. As a stationary reactor, the stator is located between the ENGINE driven IMPELLER and TURBINE. Under power, the stator redirects fluid turbulence and flow to provide impeller assist. The result is called TORQUE MULTIPLICATION. As the driven turbine begins to catch up in speed to the impeller, the stator freewheels on a SPRAG CLUTCH or ONE-WAY CLUTCH assembly.

Steering Arm. A steering arm is an arm attached to, or forged as part of, the front wheel STEERING KNUCKLE. The steering TIE ROD attaches STEERING BOX output motion to the knuckle, turning the

WHEEL to the left or right in response to STEERING WHEEL motion.

Steering Axis. Steering axis is an imaginary line formed by the near vertical centerline of the STEERING KNUCKLE, strut BALLJOINT or KINGPIN, around which a front WHEEL swings for steering.

Steering Axis Inclination (SAI). SAI is the inward tilt of the STEERING AXIS at the top, inward from the vertical as viewed from the front of the vehicle. *Also see* INCLUDED ANGLE.

Steering Box. *See* STEERING GEAR.

Steering Column. The steering column is a long housing containing the STEERING SHAFT. The STEERING WHEEL is mounted at the top of the STEERING COLUMN. The column also contains the TURN SIGNAL switch, IGNITION SWITCH, and HORN button. Some also have optional radio and speed control buttons.

Steering Gear. A steering gear is a unit located at the lower end of the STEERING SHAFT. The unit, either a recirculating-ball or rack-and-pinion design, changes the STEERING WHEEL rotary motion to linear linkage motion at the front wheel STEERING KNUCKLE. The steering gear can be manual or power assisted. *Also see* RACK-AND-PINION STEERING *and* RECIRCULATING BALL STEERING.

Steering Kickback. Steering kickback is a rapid and jerky motion of the driver's STEERING WHEEL that results as a front TIRE meets a hole or bump in the road. Steering kickback is usually caused by worn steering parts or a defective SHOCK ABSORBER.

🚌 The cause should be investigated immediately by a qualified WHEEL ALIGNMENT technician.

Steering Knuckle. The steering knuckle is the spindle center upon which a front WHEEL turns left to right, or right to left. The steering knuckle may have two BALLJOINTs or BUSHING and KINGPINS

that allow the turning action and vertical motion of the KNUCKLE upon the "A" frames or STEERING ARMS. In MACPHERSON STRUT SUSPENSIONs, the steering knuckle is fastened to, or part of, the MacPherson strut suspension assembly. To turn the knuckle, the whole STRUT is turned beneath a spring tower BEARING.

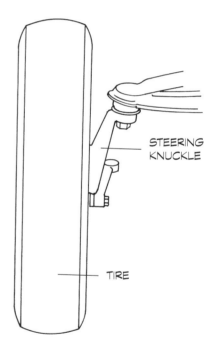

Steering Linkage. The steering linkage consists of the steering rod (if equipped), inner tie rod ends, TIE RODs, and outer tie rod ends. Vehicles containing a RACK-AND-PINION STEERING unit do not contain a steering rod.

Steering Offset. *See* SCRUB RADIUS.

Steering Ratio. The steering ratio is the degrees that the STEERING WHEEL turns in order to pivot the front wheels one degree. Some heavy vehicles having manual steering favor a slow steering ratio for its leverage. Modern POWER STEERING equipped vehicles may have a quicker ratio steering for fast steering response. The steering response ratio is determined by the relationship machined into the STEERING BOX gearing and, if equipped, the length of the STEERING ARM.

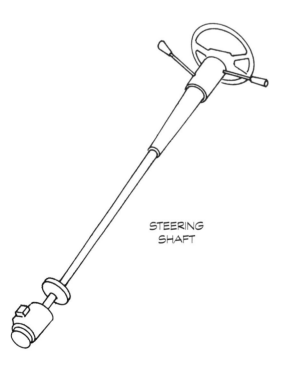

STEERING
SHAFT

Steering Shaft. The steering shaft extends from the STEERING WHEEL through the center of the STEERING COLUMN to the STEERING BOX. Usually enclosed by the column, the shaft contains a collapse sleeve or device that helps to enable column shortening in the event of vehicle collision. The lower end of the shaft sports a UNIVERSAL JOINT or RAG JOINT to mate it to the steering box.

Steering Wheel. The steering wheel is the circular-shaped wheel turned by the driver to maneuver the vehicle from straight ahead travel. Turned to the right or left, the steering wheel motion connects to the STEERING BOX and LINKAGE. The wheel's rotary motion is converted to left and right lateral motion to move the STEERING KNUCKLES at the WHEELs.

The steering wheel arms may contain buttons for operations of the HORN, CRUISE CONTROL, and possibly the vehicle radio.

Stoichiometric Fuel Ratio. An ideal air/fuel mixture of 14.7:1 (14.7 parts air to one part fuel) where all of the chemical reactants are consumed is called the stoichiometric fuel ratio. The average is aimed for when designing the air flow and FUEL system components to maintain and maximize the effect of the exhaust cleansing CATALYTIC CONVERTER action in the midst of the full air/fuel mixture range.

Stop Light. *See* BRAKE LIGHT.

Stroke. A mechanical stroke is a linear or arced distance of travel. In the engine CYLINDER, the stroke is the travel as a PISTON moves from TOP DEAD CENTER (TDC) to BOTTOM DEAD CENTER (BDC) crankshaft rotation. It is also the name given to the travel arc a windshield wiper arm makes on a windshield.

Strut. The strut is a reaction rod. The strut is sometimes also called a CONTROL ARM or LONGITUDINAL ARM. A SUSPENSION strut is simply a metal bar connecting the lower suspension control arm to the vehicle FRAME or body. Not to be confused with a MacPherson strut, the control arm is the STRUT arm that retains the BALLJOINT's outboard or inboard position as the suspension travels vertically. A longitudinal strut or arm retains the fore-and-aft position

of the lower ball joint. Depending on the positioning of the longitudinal strut or arm at the vehicle body, it may also be called a RADIUS ROD, LEADING ARM, or TRAILING ARM. Struts or arms may be part of either a front or rear suspension system, or both.

Also see MACPHERSON STRUT SUSPENSION.

Strut or arm rubber BUSHING wear usually affects CASTER and CAMBER settings. Worn bushings can cause vehicle wander, especially of bumpy roads. Bent struts can cause pulling and high rates of TIRE wear. Strut or strut bushing repairs usually require vehicle WHEEL realignment.

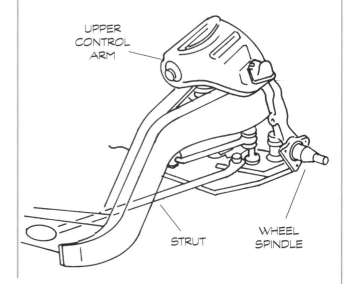

UPPER CONTROL ARM

STRUT

WHEEL SPINDLE

Subframe. An ENGINE and TRANSMISSION cradle beneath a UNIBODY vehicle that attaches to the front of the vehicle body is often termed as the subframe. A subframe is often also the cradle that contains the front wheel MacPherson struts and RACK-AND-PINION STEERING unit.

Sulfation. Sulfation is an action that can occur in a lead plate BATTERY. The sulfation that forms on a wet-cell vehicle battery PLATE as a result of the ELECTROLYTE action cannot be removed. Normally, sulfation is minimal, unless the electrolyte level decreases to expose the plate to air.

Sulfuric Acid. *See* ELECTROLYTE.

Sulfuric Oxides (SO₂). SO₂ is an acidic GAS that forms as the result of a combustion reaction. Sulfur in the FUEL combines with OXYGEN in the air. SO₂ also forms as a reaction between hot exhaust gas and the oxidizing catalyst in a CATALYTIC CONVERTER.

An overly rich fuel mixture can raise the level of this pollutant to unacceptable levels, so that a rotten egg smell emits from the vehicle ex-

haust. If this condition arises, immediate attention is necessary to restore EMISSION CONTROLs and prevent converter damage.

Sun Gear. The sun gear is the center gear of a PLANETARY GEAR-set.

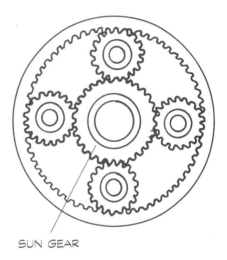

SUN GEAR

Supercharger. A supercharger is an air pump placed on a FOUR-CYCLE engine that delivers air under pressure to the intake system or engine CYLINDERs. Often called the BLOWER on TWO-CYCLE engines, the supercharger is CRANK-SHAFT-driven through GEARs or belts.

Suspension. The suspension system includes the SPRINGs, CONTROL ARMs, SHOCK ABSORBERs, and other parts that

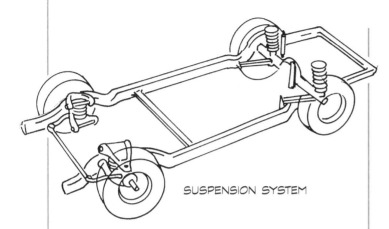

SUSPENSION SYSTEM

support the SPRUNG weight of a vehicle on axles and wheels. The suspension system is sometimes referred to as the UNSPRUNG weight of the vehicle.

Suspension Arm. *See* CONTROL ARM *and* STRUT.

Sway Bar. *See* STABILIZER BAR.

Switch. A switch is a device that opens and closes an electric CIRCUIT or VACUUM circuit. Single pole switches control only one circuit. Multiple pole or compound switches simultaneously control several circuits at once. Switches may be single throw, double throw, or rotary. Many switches may be push or pull, or electronic SENSOR devices having layered plastic contacts. Electronic sensing switches often detect heat changes

from a human finger application. Others trip as a finger breaks an optical sensor beam. The types of switches available in the automobile varies widely. Many switches, however, can be continuity tested by a technician using a high impedance multimeter.

Synchronizer. A synchronizer is a circular ring device, usually made of a brass or bronze alloy, that synchronizes GEAR speeds in a MANUAL TRANSMISSION when gear changes occur. Acting as a speed brake, the synchronizer obtains its braking pressure from the shift fork that is sliding the gear toward its mating position.

A clashing of gears, or difficulty in engagement and disengagement, may signal synchronizer wear problems. Wear normally occurs at the synchronizer teeth or braking surface. If wear is excessive, the synchronizer should be replaced.

Synthetic Oil. Synthetic oil is an OIL manufactured from alternate materials, such as agricultural products, and not a natural mineral oil made from petroleum.

Tailpipe. The tailpipe is the rearmost located EXHAUST PIPE in the EXHAUST SYSTEM. The pipe carries spent exhaust gases from the MUFFLER to the outside atmosphere. At times, a sound reducing RESONATOR like a small muffler, may grace the tailpipe toward its rearward end. The tailpipe is hung from the vehicle body or FRAME by hanger brackets. Each bracket suspends the pipe in a rubber mounting. The mountings prevent engine operating noises from transmitting to the body or frame.

Tampering. Tampering is the removing, damaging, or disconnecting of EMISSION CONTROL or safety devices on a motor vehicle to render the equipment inoperative. Though emissions and safety regulations vary according to state and federal guidelines, most require that automotive emission controls or safety devices remain in operating condition. Exceptions can be made only in specific instances, such as AIR BAG deployment which may be eliminated in some vehicles at the owner's request.

Check with an approved vehicle dealer or inspection authority before considering alterations upon any emission control or safety equipment.

Temperature Gauge. A temperature gauge is a mechanical or electronic indicator that shows the driver the temperature of the engine COOLANT.

Excess or insufficient temperature readings should receive immediate attention. However, if a vehicle temperature gauge shows a hot ENGINE condition, do not remove the RADIATOR cap to inspect the coolant. Release of radiator pressure will increase the boiling and hot coolant will erupt from the radiator filler neck. Shut the engine down, let the engine cool, and acquire the assistance of a knowledgeable and trained technician.

Thermal Vacuum Switch (TVS). A thermal vacuum switch is a VALVE that measures engine COOLANT temperature and opens or closes PORTs for the distribution of VACUUM signals in response. Used predominately with ENGINEs running carburetion, a TVS may also be called a PORTED VACUUM SWITCH (PVS).

Thermistor. A thermistor is a resistor that changes RESISTANCE value according to temperature changes. A thermistor is used for such applications as the temperature sensing device in the engine COOLANT system. A thermistor is also used to sense the air temperature that flows from an AIR CONDITIONING SYSTEM delivery duct.

Thermostat. A thermostat is a heat measurement and control device. In an engine COOLING SYSTEM, the thermostat opens and closes to regulate COOLANT flow through the ENGINE and the RADIATOR. The coolant thermostat contains a temperature sensing element that opens and closes a thermostatic VALVE. As well, a thermostat may be used by

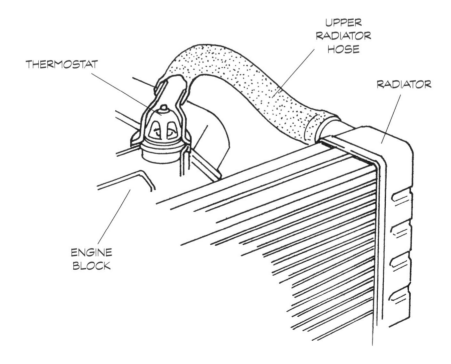

THERMOSTAT

UPPER
RADIATOR
HOSE

RADIATOR

ENGINE
BLOCK

the temperature control dial for an automatic climate control system. The desired temperature is set by driver adjustment of the thermostat, and the system automatically controls delivered blends of air to the passenger compartment.

Thermostatic Expansion Valve. *See* EXPANSION VALVE.

Thermostatic Switch. A thermostatic switch is a temperature-operated electric SWITCH used for engaging temperature sensitive equipment, such as an engine coolant FAN or air conditioning circuits. In some cycling compressor clutch A/C systems, the COMPRESSOR CLUTCH may have thermostatic switch control. The switch measures airflow temperature from the EVAPORATOR to control COMPRESSOR operation. The unit prevents humidity from freezing on the evaporator core and controls the cooling temperature of the air flowing into the passenger compartment from the evaporator.

Third Member. The third member is the final drive unit in a REAR-WHEEL DRIVE vehicle's ENGINE, TRANSMISSION, and differential DRIVELINE. The term includes the DIFFERENTIAL, AXLES, REAR HOUSING, BRAKE units, and rear WHEELS.

Throttle. The throttle controls the amount of air an ENGINE consumes. If we control the air intake of a GASOLINE engine, and control the FUEL amounts blended with the air, we control the amount of power and speed the engine can produce. However, note that DIESEL ENGINEs do not need THROTTLE PLATES. Diesels are power-controlled by the amount of fuel injected. However, some diesel engines have throttle plates so that a usable MANIFOLD VACUUM may develop.

Throttle Body. A throttle body is an airflow control for an ENGINE. Used primarily on GASOLINE engines, the throttle body is a unit that responds to gas pedal position to govern the power output and speed of the engine. The power and speed are controlled by the amount of air/fuel mixture that enters into the INTAKE MANIFOLD and engine CYLINDERs.

Throttle Body Fuel Injection (TBI). A throttle body fuel injection system is a

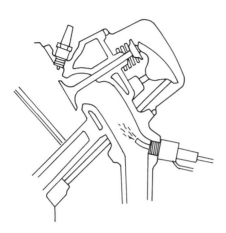

GASOLINE engine injection system that centralizes the point of FUEL introduction to the THROTTLE BODY. The injector(s) mount in the throttle body and sprays fuel under pressure into the intake air stream. TBI may also be called SINGLE POINT INJECTION (SPI) or CENTRAL FUEL INJECTION (CFI).

Throttle Plate. The throttle plate is the circular plate found in the CARBURETOR or GASOLINE injection system THROTTLE

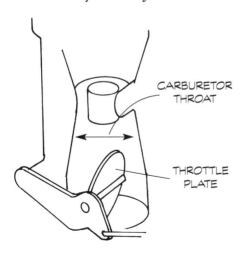

CARBURETOR THROAT

THROTTLE PLATE

BODY. The throttle plates admit air to the engine INTAKE MANIFOLD. *Also see* THROTTLE.

Throttle Position Sensor (TPS). A throttle position sensor is a variable resistance SENSOR mounted on the throttle body's THROTTLE PLATE shaft that returns a varying voltage signal to the ECM or PCM. The signal varies according to the THROTTLE VALVE opening position. The TPS may, or may not have an electrical output adjustment that calibrates the return voltage at a given throttle plate position. Among other items, the TPS signal may be used to influence FUEL INJECTION quantities, ignition spark plug TIMING, and AUTOMATIC TRANSMISSION shift points.

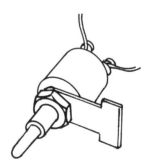

THROTTLE POSITION SWITCH

Throttle Pressure. In an AUTOMATIC TRANSMISSION, the throttle pressure is determined by engine THROTTLE opening. In older vehicles, throttle pressure is controlled by CABLE or mechanical LINKAGE. In later models, the TRANSMISSION pressure may be controlled by electronic sensing. The throttle pressure adjusts the TRANSMISSION shift points and shift firmness according to the driver's gas pedal position. Throttle pressure may also called THROTTLE VALVE pressure or TV pressure. VACUUM MODULATOR pressure may be used in some automatic transmissions instead of throttle pressure.

Throttle Valve. A throttle valve is a circular disc air VALVE in the CARBURETOR or THROTTLE BODY that opens or closes by pivoting its position in the intake air stream. The throttle valve thus varies air intake amounts in response to the driver's ACCELERATOR PEDAL position. Engine speed and power is controlled by the INTAKE MANIFOLD admission of more or less air in a DIESEL ENGINE, or air/fuel mixture in a GASOLINE engine.

Throwout Bearing. *See* RELEASE BEARING.

Thrust Angle. Thrust angle is an imaginary angle that is formed between the TRACKING centerline of the vehicle WHEELs and the true vehicle centerline. Errors in thrust angle may be created by wheel misalignment or WANDER. Measured by most modern WHEEL ALIGNMENT machines, in most vehicles, thrust angle error is a correctable setting, especially in FRONT-WHEEL DRIVE (FWD) vehicles. Though sometimes used interchangeably thrust angle differs from THRUST LINE. Thrust line is the direction the vehicle would take if the operator lets go of a centered STEERING WHEEL. Thrust angle will affect thrust line. If thrust line is incorrect the vehicle will turn, making a circle though the steering wheel remains centered.

Thrust Bearing. A thrust bearing absorbs longitudinal thrust force of a shaft. Thrust force occurs parallel to a shaft's rotational axis. The BEARING supports these axial loads, preventing excess ENDPLAY of the shaft. In the ENGINE, for example, a MAIN BEARING contains thrust faces. The thrust main bearing, therefore, controls the CRANKSHAFT's fore and aft movement within the ENGINE BLOCK.

Thrust Line. The direction the vehicle

would take if the operator lets go of a centered STEERING WHEEL. *Also see* THRUST ANGLE.

Tie Rod. A tie rod moves the STEERING KNUCKLE to the right or left as the steering system is operated by the driver. The rod pushes or pulls the steering knuckle CONTROL ARMS as the STEERING WHEEL turns.

Timing. Timing is the act of synchronizing the occurrence of events. For example, the IGNITION spark operation must by timed to coincide with the operation of the engine PISTON and cylinder VALVES. An automatic transmission CLUTCH must be timed so to prevent rapid harsh shifting at light engine THROTTLE settings, and yet timed differ-

ently for quick action during WIDE-OPEN-THROTTLE, high engine power events.

Timing Belt. A timing belt is a toothed rubber BELT that drives an engine CAMSHAFT sprocket from a CRANKSHAFT sprocket. If a timing belt jumps or fails, serious damage can be caused in certain engines. If the ENGINE has no interference relief built into the PISTON design, open ENGINE VALVES can be bent and damaged by moving pistons when the camshaft stops rotating.

Due to timing belt stretch and wear, inspection and tension adjustments must be accomplished on a regular basis. See your service technician to follow the proper belt service interval or mileage recommendations.

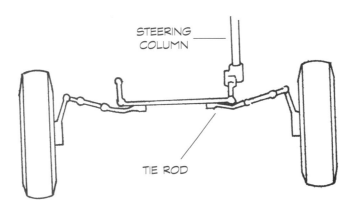

STEERING COLUMN

TIE ROD

Timing Chain. The timing chain is found in an ENGINE to keep the rotation relationship of the CAMSHAFT gear and CRANKSHAFT gear in proper sequence. If a timing chain jumps or fails, serious damage can be caused in certain engines. If the engine has no interference relief built into the PISTON design, open ENGINE VALVES can be bent and damaged by moving pistons when the camshaft stops rotating. In many engines, timing chain PLAY is not adjustable.

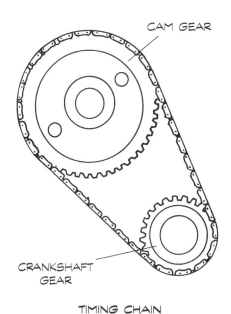

CAM GEAR

CRANKSHAFT
GEAR

TIMING CHAIN

Tire. The tire is the unit mounted on a vehicle WHEEL. In the automobile, the pneumatic tire is made of a structural casing and the TREAD body. The tire transmits traction forces to the ground or road. Basically available in inner tube or non-inner tube designs, some modern tires may include liners or materials to provide flat tire or blowout protection. Tire sizes are rated according to vehicle weight, load, and speed expectations.

 See a recommended tire dealer for replacement information.

Tire Rotation. *See* ROTATION.

Toe. Toe is the distance expressed in inches, millimeters, or degrees that front WHEELs of a vehicle point inward or outward. An incorrect toe setting tends to promote WANDER or tire tread scrub. Tire scrub usually wears the TIRE across the entire lateral TREAD surface. Scrub often leaves a sharp edge on a tread that knifes toward the toe error. If excess "toe out" exists, for example, the knife edge points toward the outside of the tire treads as mounted on the vehicle. If excess "toe in" exists the knife edge will be on the inboard portion of each tread. *See* SCRUB RADIUS.

Top Dead Center (TDC). Top Dead Center is the PISTON and CRANKSHAFT rotational position as the piston reaches the upper limit of its travel in the CYLINDER. Zero degrees TDC indicates the crankshaft's rotational point is moving from the upward movement of the pis-

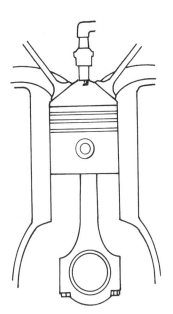

TOP DEAD CENTER

ton to the downward movement transition, and the CONNECTING ROD centerline position parallels the cylinder walls.

Torque. Torque is a twisting or turning energy force.

Torque Converter. Used in most AUTO-

MATIC TRANSMISSIONs, the torque converter is a FLUID COUPLING incorporating three sets of VANE blades: the IMPELLER, STATOR, and TURBINE. The motive power transfers from the engine-driven impeller to the turbine via the transmission fluid thrown by the impeller. The laws of fluid motion, called hydrodynamics, allow that the fluid strikes the turbine to exert impact force on its blades. The turbine connects to transmission INPUT SHAFT. As the fluid strikes the turbine, the force attempts to move the turbine and transmission input shaft.

When great speed differences exist between the impeller and turbine speed, as occurs when the engine pro-

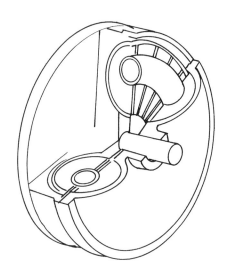

TORQUE CONVERTER

duces sufficient power to accelerate the vehicle, the impeller throws the fluid at the turbine with high amounts of force. The fluid deflects in the turbine and expends its energy. As the fluid loses momentum, it loses centrifugal force and flows inward toward the stator vanes. The fluid impact locks the stator on its SPRAG CLUTCH (or ONE-WAY CLUTCH). The stator thereby cannot freewheel. The stator thus redirects the fluid toward the direction of engine rotation. This redirection produces an effect called TORQUE MULTIPLICATION.

As the vehicle accelerates to cruising speed, the turbine almost catches the impeller speed. As this occurs at vehicle cruising, the stator CLUTCH unlocks to permit stator rotation in concert with the other two elements.

In a converter, three predominant malfunctions may occur:

■ The stator clutch fails. Failure of the stator lock provides poor performance. Also, often a sprag clutch or one-way clutch mechanically breaks and its metal particles pollute the entire transmission fluid circuit.

■ The stator won't freewheel. The stator won't be carried along with the impeller and turbine at cruising TORQUE.

The stator thus holds the two units back and cruising power and speed ability is lost. FUEL economy suffers. Usually the turbulence created generates a great amount of heat from the converter. The heat may damage the automatic transmission.

■ The torque converter leaks. Leakage usually occurs at the converter to front transmission SEAL. Sometimes a leak will occur at converter welds or bolts. Remember, the torque converter must remain filled to operate properly. A failed converter drainback protection VALVE may overfill the transmission fluid sump during times when the engine is shut off, and halt torque converter operation when the vehicle engine first starts.

Torque converter diagnosis should be part of a comprehensive automatic transmission diagnosis. See your vehicle manufacturer or a competent transmission repair specialist.

Torque Converter Clutch (TCC). A torque converter clutch is a unit in a TORQUE CONVERTER that can engage and lock the engine crankshaft and transmission INPUT SHAFT. The CLUTCH eliminates the slipping loss that is normal through the torque converter at vehicle cruising. Normally, the torque converter clutch avoids about 5 to 10 percent speed loss through the torque converter. In many instances, this unit is considered erroneously as an OVER-DRIVE unit. Depending on the torque converter design, the TCC may or may not be a serviceable item.

Torque Multiplication. Torque multiplication is the mechanical advantage gained by using a TORQUE CONVERTER or gear reduction. The converter or GEAR allows a gain in power by sacrifice of speed (r.p.m.).

Torsional Vibration. Rotary roughness in motion that causes an uneven force on part of a shaft to repeatedly move ahead or lag behind the shaft remainder is called torsional vibration. In an ENGINE, torsional vibration can be caused by CYLINDER misfire or component imbalance. Minor torsional vibration is absorbed by the VIBRATION DAMPER mounted on the engine CRANK-SHAFT.

Torsion Bar. A torsion bar is a straight bar, made of metal or other material, that is fastened solidly at one end and allowed to twist at the other end. In vehicle SUSPENSION, the torsion bar fas-

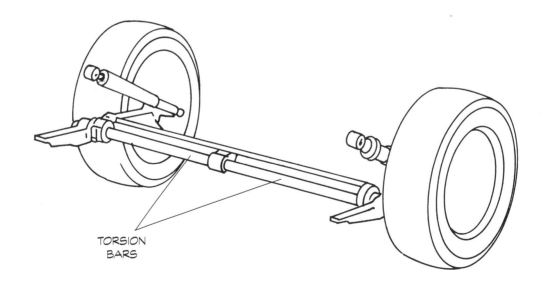

TORSION BARS

tens to the vehicle body or FRAME at one end, and supports the vehicle in its fastening under tension to the CONTROL ARM or "A" frame at the other end. Spring action occurs as the twisting bar flexes as the control arm BALLJOINT end moves up and down. Some vehicles contain a common bar to support both left and right suspensions together. Others contain a bar for each WHEEL. Torsion bars may be used in front or rear suspensions, or both.

Tracking. Tracking is the alignment factor that dictates handling so that the vehicle rear WHEELs follow centered behind the front wheels. *Also see* THRUST ANGLE.

Traction Control. A traction control is a TORQUE control system that uses vehicle BRAKE applications to prevent unwanted WHEEL spin during vehicle acceleration. Usually integrated with an ANTILOCK BRAKE SYSTEM (ABS), the traction control allows the ABS brake computer or control to apply the BRAKE LINING of a wheel that rotates at a marked differing speed to the other wheels. This action reduces the tendency toward wheel spin on slippery surfaces.

Trailing Arm. The trailing arm is a suspension CONTROL ARM that extends toward the rear of the vehicle. The arm fastens to the SUSPENSION at its forward end, and through a BUSHING to the body or FRAME at its rearward end.

Transaxle. A transaxle is a component that performs the duties of both TRANSMISSION and DIFFERENTIAL or AXLE. Used mostly in FRONT-WHEEL DRIVE vehicles, the transaxle attaches via a bell housing to one end of the ENGINE and passes engine TORQUE through the transmission portion of the transaxle to the DRIVE WHEELS.

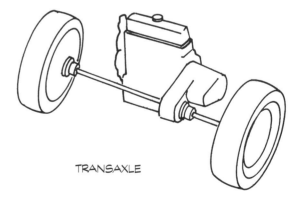

TRANSAXLE

Transfer Case. A transfer case is an auxiliary TRANSMISSION mounted behind the main transmission assembly on FOUR-

WHEEL DRIVE or ALL-WHEEL DRIVE vehicles. The transfer case allows a dividing of power flow so that TORQUE can drive both front and rear DIFFERENTIALs, either full-time or part-time. A transfer case may contain GEARs or a chain drive assembly. The transfer case may use gear OIL or automatic transmission fluid for lubrication.

See your vehicle manufacturer or repair technician for service details.

Transistor. A transistor is a semiconductor device that controls the flow of ELECTRIC CURRENT. The transistor usually acts as an electrical SWITCH or an amplifier.

Transmission. A transmission is a unit that contains shafts, GEARs, and other parts, used to transmit TORQUE to a DRIVESHAFT. In the automobile, the DRIVELINE transmission provides neutral, reverse, and various forward GEAR RATIOs. Usually driven via a CLUTCH or TORQUE CONVERTER, the transmission may be manual, automatic, or continuously variable. In a windshield wiper or door glass application, the transmis-

sion may be a simple gear device to provide forward or reverse LINKAGE movements.

Transmission Control Module (TCM). The transmission control module controls the shifting action of the AUTOMATIC TRANSMISSION, tailoring the action to ENGINE power output, vehicle speed, and EMISSION CONTROL parameters. This unit may work in conjunction with a POWERTRAIN CONTROL MODULE (PCM) and VEHICLE CONTROL MODULE (VCM).

Tread. The tread is the TIRE portion that contacts the ground or road. The tread has a traction pattern molded into its face. Various tread patterns are available to suit the tire for the type of driving the vehicle encounters. Depending on the tread pattern and the rubber composition of the tread, the

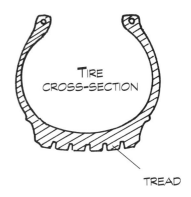

TIRE
CROSS-SECTION

TREAD

expected mileage life of the tread varies. More aggressive, or open tread patterns are usually reserved for off-road and mud or snow driving.

Trigger. A trigger is a signal or the signaling unit used to activate a component or cause an event. For example, a magnetic crankshaft position SENSOR may trigger the operation of fuel injectors and SPARK PLUG firings on a modern GASOLINE engine.

Trouble Codes. On OBD-equipped vehicles, trouble codes are electrical encoded signals stored by computer that are read by a technician to guide repair processes. Trouble codes can be retrieved and read by a qualified, trained technician with a diagnostic tester. Trouble codes are often referred to as DIAGNOSTIC TROUBLE CODEs, or DTCs.

Tune-up. The tune-up is an inspection, testing, and adjustment of a vehicle POWERTRAIN to ensure low emissions and good vehicle performance.

See your vehicle manufacturer or service technician for inspection and service intervals.

Tuned Port Injection. A tuned port injection system combines FUEL INJECTION with the advantages of INTAKE MANIFOLD airflow tuning. Airflow tuning increases engine performance by the virtue of air echoes that supercharge the ENGINE at specific revolutions per minute (r.p.m.). *Also see* PORT FUEL INJECTION (PFI).

Turbine. The turbine is the power-receiving blade unit of a centrifugal air or liquid pump. The air or fluid thrown to the turbine by the IMPELLER expends mass weight against the turbine blades. In response the turbine blades may rotate the turbine assembly. The turbine is therefore the driven part of a FLUID COUPLING or TORQUE CONVERTER.

Turbocharger. A turbocharger is a centrifugal air pump that is driven by the engine exhaust gas energy. The turbocharger BOOST, therefore responds to engine load and speed. The boost increases engine performance by stuffing the CYLINDERS with pressurized air. The COMPRESSION and COMBUSTION pressures are therefore raised higher than those of a normally aspirated ENGINE. The unit, raises the need for adequate engine cooling and high-performance parts within the engine.

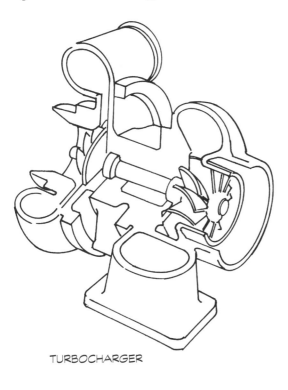

TURBOCHARGER

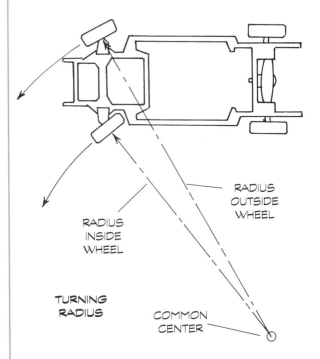

RADIUS
OUTSIDE
WHEEL

RADIUS
INSIDE
WHEEL

TURNING
RADIUS

COMMON
CENTER

Check your service manual or dealer for turbocharged engine maintenance recommendations.

Turning Radius. The turning radius is the distance that a WHEEL takes from the center of the turn when the STEERING WHEEL is turned a stated number of degrees to the left or right. The turning radius differs whether the front wheel is an outboard or inboard wheel in the turn. The STEERING LINKAGE dimensions accommodate the needed change, as long as the linkage is not worn or bent. Since the outer wheel needs to turn less to make the circle, this normal dimension is called "toe out" on turns. A left-to-right comparison may signal errors that point toward steering linkage troubles.

Turn Signal. A turn signal is a directional signal lamp located at the front and rear of a vehicle. Illuminated by a combination bulb, the turn signal shares bulb operation with the PARKING

LIGHTs. The turn signal operates from a switch located on the STEERING COLUMN. An electrical unit called a FLASHER gives the turn signal a blinking effect for warning.

TV. *See* THROTTLE VALVE.

Two-Cycle. A two-cycle ENGINE receives intake as the cylinder COMBUSTION pushes the PISTON down past low ports within the cylinder wall. The incoming intake air drives the exhaust gasses out of the CYLINDER. COMPRESSION occurs in the upward piston stroke, and FUEL firing occurs near TOP DEAD CENTER (TDC).

Though it produces a large amount of low r.p.m. TORQUE, the two-cycle engine has a greater propensity to produce air pollution than a FOUR STROKE engine. Also often called the TWO-STROKE engine, with only a few historical exceptions the two-cycle engine has not been widely used in automobiles.

Two-Stroke. A two-stroke engine is a design that contains only two PISTON strokes for the occurrence of the complete four cycles of engine breathing and COMBUSTION. However, since the two-stroke engine generates more heat in less time, and usually emits greater pollution from its combustion, it is not generally used in automobiles.

Two-Wheel Drive. Two-wheel drive is an automotive propulsion system that uses only two of the four vehicle WHEELs to provide motive power to the road.

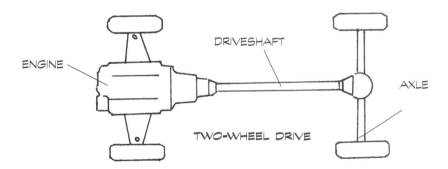

ENGINE

DRIVESHAFT

AXLE

TWO-WHEEL DRIVE

Unibody. The unibody is a vehicle body and FRAME welded together in unitized fashion. Most modern automobiles are unibody construction. This type of vehicle design incorporates the use of high-strength steel for strength while also saving on vehicle weight. The net result is a lighter and more FUEL efficient automobile. If body repairs are to be made to a unibody vehicle, an adequate repair may involve measuring, straightening, and welding techniques particularly suited to this type of vehicle design.

Universal Joint. A universal joint is a DRIVELINE joint that allows the transmission of TORQUE from one shaft to another through a minor angle in relation to each other. *Also see* CONSTANT VELOCITY UNIVERSAL JOINT.

Unsprung. The unsprung weight of a vehicle is the portion of the CHASSIS and SUSPENSION not supported by the SPRINGS. Suspension components, BRAKE parts, HUBS, WHEEL BEARINGS, WHEELS, and TIRES are among the unsprung weight components of a vehicle.

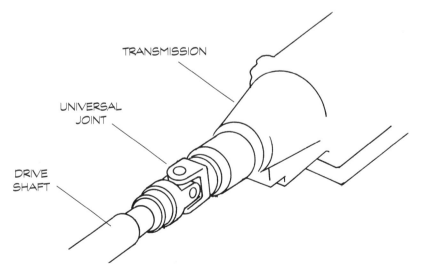

TRANSMISSION

UNIVERSAL JOINT

DRIVE SHAFT

Vacuum. In an automobile, vacuum indicates any air pressure below atmospheric pressure. The energy potential found in the differences in air pressure may be used to do work. For example, to stop a vehicle, a vacuum brake BOOSTER may assist the driver's foot effort on the BRAKE PEDAL.

Vacuum Advance. Used in older vehicles, the vacuum advance performed the advancing of ignition TIMING. The timing would adjust in response to INTAKE MANIFOLD vacuum caused primarily by the THROTTLE PLATE opening and ENGINE load.

Vacuum Modulator. *See* MODULATOR VALVE.

Vacuum Modulator Canister. The vacuum modulator canister is a cylindrical chamber that contains a vacuum DIAPHRAGM and its attending modulator rod. Responding to VACUUM signals upon the diaphragm, the rod move-ment controls the position of an automatic transmission MODULATOR VALVE. The valve varies transmission CLUTCH and BAND apply pressures and road speed shift points, to accommodate engine TORQUE changes.

Some modulator canisters may contain a bellows chamber so that altitude compensation automatically occurs. If a modulator fails, the TRANSMISSION fluid pressure usually rises very high. The high pressure usually causes shift points to occur very late in speed and feel very firm.

Vacuum Motor. A vacuum motor is a MOTOR that uses the differences between a stored VACUUM and a pressure to accomplish a task. Usually powered by INTAKE MANIFOLD vacuum kept in a vacuum chamber, a vacuum motor moves a diaphragm-attached device in response to changes in the applied vacuum. The vacuum application is often controlled through a port SWITCH. A vacuum motor is used in many applications. For example, a vacuum motor may operate a FOUR WHEEL DRIVE (4WD) engagement, or may control the movements of an air conditioning airflow door. If the vacuum signal is deficient from the ENGINE, or the air is allowed to leak into the system, the operation of a vacuum-powered unit will suffer or cease.

Vacuum Sensor. *See* MAP SENSOR.

Vacuum Solenoid Valve (VSV). A VSV is used to control the purging cycle of the CHARCOAL CANISTER. After the ENGINE warms-up, the VSV receives a signal to open the purge circuit. The VSV opening allows accumulated FUEL TANK vapors to purge from the charcoal to the engine intake system. The VSV is often referred to as the PURGE VALVE.

Vacuum Switch. A vacuum switch controls the flow of VACUUM by opening or closing PORTs. Also, a vacuum switch is an electrical SWITCH that operates an electrical signal in response to changes in an applied vacuum.

Valve. A valve is a flow control device that opens or closes. The valve con-

trols the flow of a gas pressure or liquid. In an ENGINE, the CYLINDER HEAD valves control the flow of air, FUEL, and exhaust gases through the COMBUSTION cycle.

Valve Body. A valve body is a casting in the automatic transmission OIL PAN that houses VALVEs for the HYDRAULIC control of an AUTOMATIC TRANSMISSION. The valve body is an intricate unit that responds to MANIFOLD VACUUM, THROTTLE PLATE changes, road speed input, and GEAR range selection. The valves operating within the valve body may function in response to VACUUM, mechanical linkage, air or fluid pressures, or electrical solenoid signals.

Because of its complexity, services to a valve body should only be accomplished by trained automatic transmission specialists.

Valve Clearance. Used in the ENGINE, valve clearance is the mechanical GAP used to allow for heat expansion of the ENGINE VALVE and VALVETRAIN. Valve clearance is measured when the valve is closed and the CAMSHAFT operating lobe is positioned on its base circle.

Some vehicles may incorporate a mechanical valve clearance. This mechanical type usually offers some operating noise until the engine warms and takes up excess cold clearance with metal expansion.

In valvetrain designs having hydraulic LIFTER or FOLLOWER, the clearance runs at ZERO. The clearance is automatically taken up by OIL pressure routed through the valve lifter or follower.

If a valve clicks or taps, repairs may be needed to repair valvetrain components.

Valve Guide. A valve guide is a cylindrical hole in the CYLINDER HEAD that allows the longitudinal operation of the cylinder VALVE. Often subjected to high wear if high engine heat or OIL deposits lower the available lubrication, a defective guide may impair proper seating and sealing of the VALVE. Valve seating failure causes a CYLINDER misfire through a loss of cylinder COMPRESSION.

Repairs to the engine valve guide usually requires cylinder head removal and machine shop services.

Valve Head. The valve head is the largest part of the ENGINE VALVE that nestles into the CYLINDER HEAD seat when the valve is closed. The valve head contains an angled machined surface called the VALVE SEAT that promotes good sealing when tightly closed with VALVE SPRING tension.

Valve Lifter. A valve lifter is the cylindrical metal part that transmits CAM LOBE rotation into longitudinal movement of the engine VALVETRAIN and VALVE. In OVERHEAD VALVE (OHV) engines, the LIFTER push causes the ROCKER ARM to

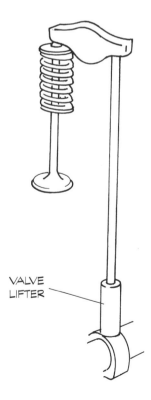

VALVE
LIFTER

lever and open the valve. The lifter may be a mechanical or solid metal unit, roller, or a HYDRAULIC unit. *Also see* VALVE CLEARANCE.

Valve Overlap. Valve overlap is the degrees of CRANKSHAFT rotation wherein the cylinder EXHAUST VALVE is closing and the INTAKE VALVE is lifting from its seat. Valve overlap is closely tailored so that the momentum of the exhaust gases help to scavenge the CYLINDER of spent exhaust while helping to start intake air/fuel flow. To cut HYDROCARBON fuel losses, some injection systems time the FUEL INJECTIONs to occur after the exhaust valve closes completely.

Valve Seat. The valve seat is the surface upon which the VALVE rests when the valve closes. During INTAKE VALVE seating, the intake valve seat prevents flow of COMPRESSION back into the INTAKE MANIFOLD. During EXHAUST VALVE seating, the exhaust valve seat shuts the door on INTAKE STROKE air/fuel mixture losses into the EXHAUST SYSTEM. To do their tasks, seat concentricity must be true to the VALVE HEAD sealing surfaces. Also, the valves and seats must remain clean from CARBON deposits. Lack of proper

seat sealing can cause CYLINDER pressure losses and valve burning.

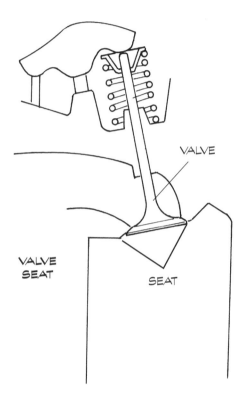

Valve Seat Insert. A valve seat insert is a metal ring that is often installed in the engine CYLINDER HEAD to provide a VALVE SEAT. Often used as a repair technique for engines that burn VALVE HEADs and severely damage valve seats, primarily the replacement seat is temperature fit into the head. The head is heated, and the valve seat insert is chilled before a tight fit insertion. After the two units normalize in temperature, the new valve seat insert is effectively part of the cylinder head. After installation, the new valve seat can be machined to accept the new valve head sealing surface.

Valve Spring. A valve spring is a COIL spring that closes each ENGINE VALVE. Attached to the valve and secured by the valve spring retainer and keeper, the SPRING closes the valve after the CAM LOBE rotates past the open valve position. Weak or broken springs can cause COMPRESSION loss and misfire due to VALVE bounce or float.

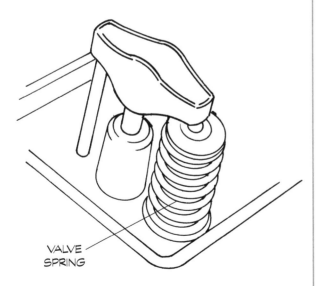

VALVE
SPRING

Valve Tappet. *See* VALVE LIFTER.

Valve Timing. Valve timing is the opening and closing of ENGINE VALVEs in relation to the CRANKSHAFT and PISTON positions. Expressed in crankshaft degrees, the valve timing is very important to efficient ENGINE breathing, power, and EMISSION CONTROLS.

Valvetrain. The valvetrain parts mechanically open and close the ENGINE valves. The valvetrain transfers CAM LOBE rotation to the longitudinal movement at the valves. Valvetrain components may include the LIFTER or FOLLOWER, PUSHROD, ROCKER ARM, and the VALVE.

Vane. A vane is a flat blade that is turned in circular fashion by a HUB. Sometimes spring-loaded to maintain a SEAL with an outer ring, a vane is used in SUPERCHARGERS, TURBOCHARGERS, or other air pumps. Vanes are also used in pumps for TRANSMISSION fluid and engine COOLANT pumps.

Vane Airflow Meter. Used in the ENGINE intake airflow system of many early ELECTRONIC FUEL INJECTION (EFI) systems, the vane airflow meter used a spring

loaded movable vane door to measure engine air intake. The vane airflow meter plate or flap connected to a variable resistor. The resistor therefore returned a voltage signal to the fuel injection computer based upon the amount of air flowing into the engine. The FUEL INJECTION amounts were partly based on this electrical information.

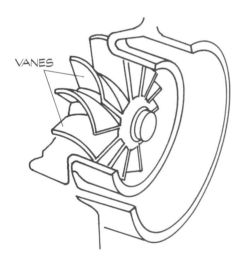

VANES

VANES IN A TURBOCHARGER

Vapor Lock. Boiling of the FUEL in the fuel system caused by excess heat is called vapor lock. In the FUEL LINES, vapor lock would hamper the pumping action of a spring-diaphragm FUEL PUMP of a carbureted ENGINE. Also in carbureted engines, CARBURETOR boiling

would raise the vapor pressure within the carburetor fuel metering circuits, and the engine would flood from excess fuel flow. Vapor lock is not usually a condition that often hampers a fuel injected engine, due to the higher injection system fuel pressures.

Vehicle Control Module. A vehicle control module is a computer that operates in conjunction with a POWERTRAIN CONTROL MODULE and BODY CONTROL MODULE to monitor and control various aspects of the modern vehicle operation.

Vehicle Identification Number (VIN). The VIN is the encoded number assigned to each vehicle by the vehicle manufacturer. The VIN normally contains numerically and alphabetically coded sequences that identify various vehicle components.

⚠ Do not alter the VIN number. A VIN must be recognized by the state of vehicle licensure. VIN alteration or reissue is an official procedure usually reserved for vehicles that are reclaimed after major collision damage has occurred.

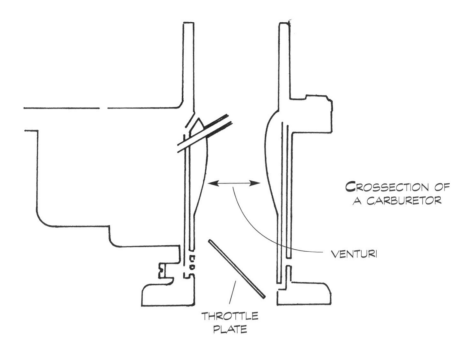

CROSSECTION OF
A CARBURETOR

VENTURI

THROTTLE
PLATE

Venturi. A Venturi is a restrictive narrowing within the throat of a CARBURETOR or THROTTLE BODY that develops VACUUM as air passes through. In carburetors, the vacuum allows atomized FUEL to flow into the intake air stream. In both a carburetor or throttle body, the Venturi vacuum signal may also be tapped for the operation of various vacuum SERVOS or MOTORS, such as the VACUUM ADVANCE mechanism of an IGNITION DISTRIBUTOR.

Vibration Damper. A vibration damper (also DAMPENER) is a balancing device that attaches to one end of the engine CRANKSHAFT. The vibration damper reduces the torsional vibrations within the crankshaft metal. The vibrations are caused by CYLINDER firing impulses. The vibration damper may also be called the HARMONIC BALANCER.

Viscosity. A liquid's resistance to flow is called its viscosity. Thicker lubricating OIL has greater viscosity than a thin oil. Oil is rated by viscosity weight by the Society of Automotive Engineers (SAE). Engine oils usually range between 5W for thin, to 40W for thicker oil. Multiple viscosity oils are rated such as 10W-40. The "W" stands for the cold (winter) properties of the oil. This indicates that the oil replicates a thin oil (10W) at cold temperatures, and a thicker oil (40W) at hot temperatures.

Viscous Clutch. A viscous clutch is a coupling similar in operation to the TORQUE CONVERTER. The viscous clutch is used in DRIVETRAIN applications to operate TRANSMISSION components, or automatically transfer power in a DIFFERENTIAL to non-slipping wheels if a WHEEL loses traction. The viscous clutch is often also used in a cooling system FAN clutch.

In the COOLING SYSTEM, the unit responds to the application of air temperatures coming through the RADIATOR, declutching the fan at cool airflow periods. This action saves FUEL consumption during times that radiator airflow assistance is not needed.

Volatility. Volatility is the measure used to describe the ease of liquid evaporation. Volatility is an expression of the FUEL's flammability. GASOLINE has a greater volatility than DIESEL FUEL. Therefore gasoline evaporates more rapidly and ignites more easily than diesel fuel.

Volt. A volt is an electrical measurement that describes the electrical pressure needed to push one AMPERE through one OHM of RESISTANCE.

Voltmeter. A voltmeter measures the voltage potential between points in an electric CIRCUIT. In automotive work, the voltmeter shows the voltage present in the ALTERNATOR output, across the BATTERY, or in various points of a wiring circuit. In modern automobile electrical work, the voltmeter is likely part of a multimeter, designed so that its RESISTANCE (impedance) will not harm transistorized and computerized circuitry.

Voltage Regulator. A voltage regulator is a device that controls ALTERNATOR or GENERATOR voltage output. Usually tran-

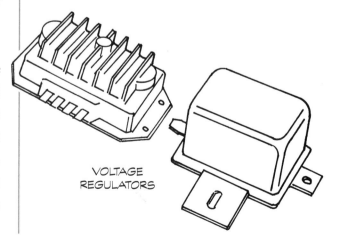

VOLTAGE
REGULATORS

sistorized in today's vehicles, the voltage regulator is usually not adjustable and may be housed inside the alternator unit.

Volume Air Flow Sensor. *See* AIR FLOW CONTROL.

Volumetric Efficiency. Volumetric efficiency is the measure of CYLINDER filling in an ENGINE. Volumetric efficiency relates to the air pumping abilities of the engine. Therefore, it relates with the engine's ability to produce power.

Vortex. A vortex is the movement of a GAS or fluid in a circular motion. Vortex COMBUSTION CHAMBER designs assist in mixing the air/fuel mixture in the CYLINDER combustion chamber and helping vaporization. The turbulent mixing helps to ensure the burning of HYDROCARBON molecules, resulting in greater engine power and lower emissions.

Wander. A wander is a vehicle drift to the right and left when the steering wheel is held stationary. Wander differs from pulling in that wander is bidirectional. Wandering can be caused by loose steering or SUSPENSION components, lack of proper toe-in or toe-out, inadequate STEERING BOX preload, insufficient positive CASTER setting, or poor TIRE tracking.

WANKEL ENGINE

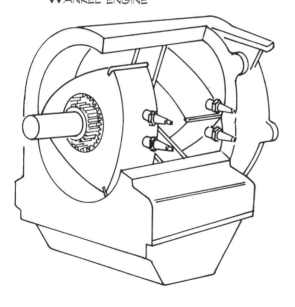

Wankel. A Wankel ROTARY ENGINE, named after its inventor, normally contains two three-lobe ROTORs. The rotors spin eccentrically in oval chambers. The effect closely resembles the combustion sequence of TWO-CYCLE engines. Wankel engines have received only scattered use in automotive applications.

Wastegate. A wastegate is a device on a TURBOCHARGER that controls output BOOST pressure by venting the driving exhaust pressures. The wastegate limits INTAKE MANIFOLD supercharging, thereby helping to prevent ENGINE and TURBOCHARGER failure.

Water Jacket. The water jacket is the space for COOLANT to flow through an automobile ENGINE. Formed by the engine's inner and outer metal structures, the water jacket allows cooling of the CYLINDERs and head(s).

Water Pump. The water pump is a liquid centrifugal pumping device that circulates engine COOLANT through the engine WATER JACKET, hoses, and RADIATOR. A water pump is usually driven by a DRIVE BELT from the engine CRANKSHAFT.

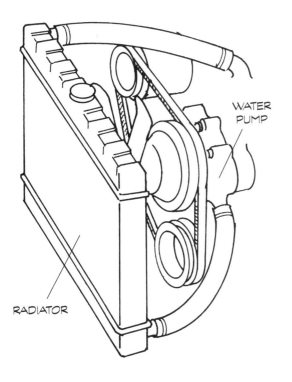

WATER PUMP

RADIATOR

Wear Sensor. A wear sensor is the tab protruding on a DISC BRAKE pad that causes squealing sounds when the brake pad wears thin.

Brakes should be serviced when the wear sensor contacts the brake ROTOR (or sooner).

Wheel. A wheel is the metal disc at the center of an automotive TIRE. The wheel, or rim, provides a seating area for the tire beads and a VALVE for tire inflation. The wheel attaches to the HUB using various studs or lugs and the wheel nuts. The nuts must be torqued in proper sequence to reduce a wheel's lateral RUNOUT.

Wheels should be balanced, rotated, and aligned on a regular basis. See your vehicle manufacturer or service technician for inspection and service intervals.

Wheel Alignment. The wheel alignment is a test of angles made to the automobile suspension and steering system. A four-wheel alignment, a standard for most of today's vehicles, includes tests for front CASTER, CAMBER, TOE, INCLUDED ANGLE, STEERING AXIS INCLINATION, and also rear toe TRACKING, and rear wheel camber.

Testing and adjusting ensures that the vehicle wheels and tires are properly positioned for good vehicle handling and maximum TIRE life. See your vehicle manufacturer or service technician for inspection and service intervals.

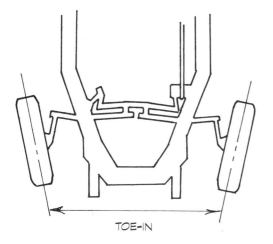

TOE-IN

WHEEL ALIGNMENT

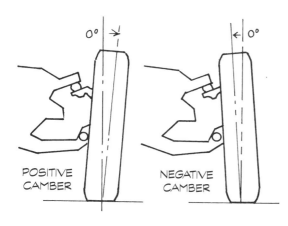

POSITIVE CAMBER

NEGATIVE CAMBER

Wheel Balancer. A wheel balancer is a machine that checks the WHEEL and TIRE assembly for imbalance. An imbalance can be static or dynamic (as the wheel spins), or both. If a wheel imbalance is detected, weights are added to the wheel to attain balance, proper balance helps prevent wheel bounce, steering wear, and tire TREAD wear called cupping.

Wheelbase. Wheelbase is the linear distance between imaginary centerlines that run across the front and rear AXLES. A comparison between left and right wheelbase dimensions may help detect a WHEEL ALIGNMENT problem.

Wheel Bearing. A wheel bearing unit is housed at the HUB of the WHEEL assembly. Depending on the year and model of the vehicle, the wheel bearing sets, either inner or outer, may be either ball or roller design. The BEARING allows high-speed rotation of the wheel and BRAKE DRUM or BRAKE DISC.

Each wheel bearing demands a quality lubricant, and a given running CLEARANCE or installation preload. Wheel bearings should be serviced at intervals mandated by the vehicle manufacturer.

Wheel Cylinder. A wheel cylinder is a

hydraulic CYLINDER mounted on the DRUM BRAKE backing plate. The wheel cylinder operates the brake SHOES when the BRAKE PEDAL is depressed. HYDRAULIC PRESSURE received from the MASTER CYLINDER pushes the wheel cylinder pistons. The PISTONS (and PUSHRODS if equipped) push outward and force the BRAKE LINING to contact the drum.

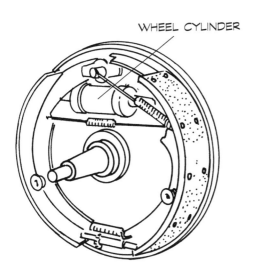

WHEEL CYLINDER

If a wheel cylinder leaks hydraulic BRAKE FLUID, the brake shoes often become contaminated (requiring replacement), and the master cylinder may cease to operate correctly.

Wide-Open-Throttle or WOT. A condition when the ENGINE is operated at maximum THROTTLE.

Wiring Harness. A wiring harness is a bundle of individually insulated wires that are wrapped and routed together. The harness, normally divided into front, INSTRUMENT PANEL, and rear sections, forms the wiring CIRCUITs for the automobile.

Wrist Pin. *See* PISTON PIN.

X-Rotation. The rotation of a vehicle's TIRE to the opposite side and opposing WHEEL position. For example, taking the left front tire and swapping it in location with the right rear tire, and doing the same action with the right front and left rear tires, is doing an x-rotation. Depending on tire design, x-rotation may or may not be recommended.

Check with your service technician or tire dealer for recommendations.

Yoke. A yoke is a section of a shaft made to accommodate a UNIVERSAL JOINT or sliding longitudinal SPLINE. *Also see* SLIP JOINT.

YOKE ON UNIVERSAL JOINT

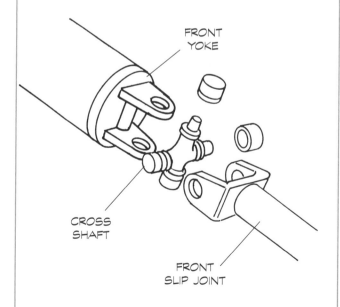

FRONT
YOKE

CROSS
SHAFT

FRONT
SLIP JOINT

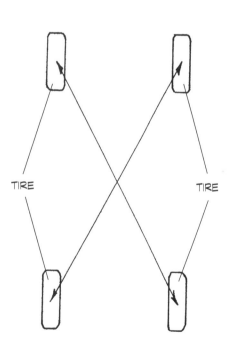

TIRE   TIRE

X-ROTATION

Zap. Zap is the sound made when inappropriate low-resistance electrical connections are made. A zap can occur if a SHORT CIRCUIT is made between the two DC connections of a vehicle's BATTERY. Sparks usually fly and wire melting can occur. The risk of battery explosion is high.

Zap is also a descriptive term used by automotive technicians to describe the effect poor vehicle maintenance has on the owner's wallet or purse. An owner's treasury is often the victim of zap by vehicle breakdowns due to service neglect.

Zener Diodes. Found in the alternator or voltage regulator, Zener diodes limit high-energy spikes to harmless levels.

Zero. A zero condition is a state of value balance between the POSITIVE and NEGATIVE. Zero is used in a vehicle WHEEL ALIGNMENT to depict the true vertical. Zero is also used by technicians to calibrate measurement instruments. For example, an OHMMETER, which measures RESISTANCE, may need to be "zeroed" before use so that its scale reads accurately.

INDEX